THE
ITALIAN
WAY

THE
ITALIAN
WAY

CELEBRATE THE FOOD, CULTURE,
ART, AND BEAUTY OF ITALY

CONTENTS

WELCOME TO ITALY

The whole world is under Italy's spell. Every year, almost 60 million of us visit to soak up that inimitable Italian charm—and who can blame us? With a history stretching back to the ancient Romans and beyond, the country has more UNESCO World Heritage Sites than anywhere else in the world. Its esteemed galleries and grand palazzos house Renaissance masterpieces that changed the face of Western art. It has over 1,500 shimmering lakes, three soaring mountain ranges, and Europe's only active volcanoes. And that's without touching on the food— the country's beloved menu has enriched every corner of the world.

The simple truth is, we're all in love with the Italian way. We wear Italian fashion, we eat Italian dishes, we drive Italian cars, and we lose ourselves in Italian cinema. The country's name alone conjures images of pure, swoon-worthy beauty: rolling Tuscan hills

dotted with olive groves, gondolas drifting serenely down Venetian canals, and steaming slices of pizza served in a streetside trattoria. This love affair with Italy is nothing new, of course; the country's majestic landscapes and rich traditions have been wooing travelers since the days of the Grand Tour.

The Italian Way is here to celebrate this cultural colossus. We've condensed the country's many charms into six themed chapters, covering everything from ancient monuments to beloved dishes to chic fashion staples. Eager to find out what happened in Caravaggio's final years, how Italians invented the beach vacation as we know it, or the right way to decode an Italian menu? All is revealed within these pages. By the book's end, you'll be clamoring to arrange your next Italian adventure. We'll see you there.

HISTORY
AND HERITAGE

◆◆◆◆◆◆◆◆◆◆◆◆◆

Italy's history hasn't just defined Italy.
From the ancient architecture of the
Romans to the iconic art of the Renaissance,
this country's cultural heritage has shaped
the modern world as we know it. You
can thank the Romans for your underfloor
heating and our world's modern calendar,
and Galileo for our understanding of
astronomy and physics, for starters.
Spanning the breadth of art, architecture,
and science, Italy has a legacy like no
other—and it's not over yet. Renaissance
techniques continue to influence
contemporary painters, Roman ruins
inspire the architects of today, and the
country's myths and legends still shape our
modern stories. This rich heritage, born
from creative thinkers and inspired leaders,
has set the scene for centuries to come.
So to understand what really makes
Italy click, there's no better place to
start than its past.

ICONIC CITIES

As the Roman Empire collapsed, the Italian peninsula reinvented itself as a collection of city-states. Florence gave birth to the Renaissance, Genova and Venice ruled the seas, Bologna founded Europe's oldest university, Naples became a center of the Baroque, and Rome solidified itself as the home of the Catholic Church. When Italy finally reemerged as a unified country in 1871, centuries of city-state solipsism had produced a country of stark divisions. Yet for many—Italians included—that's what makes Italy's cities so special.

Turin

The hub of Italian unification and the country's first capital, today Turin is best known for its regal architecture; industrial heritage (FIAT was founded here); and its rich, buttery cuisine that looks more toward Paris than Rome.

Milan

Though a major player in the Renaissance—Leonardo da Vinci painted his *Last Supper* here—Milan is best known today as Italy's industrial powerhouse, home to its stock exchange, fashion industry, and many of its leading multinational companies.

Florence

This is where the Renaissance was born, cradled, and grew up. Despite the rampant (over)tourism, the spellbinding beauty of the city endures, and a clutch of prestigious universities, institutes, and manufacturing firms ensures the city is not just a theme park.

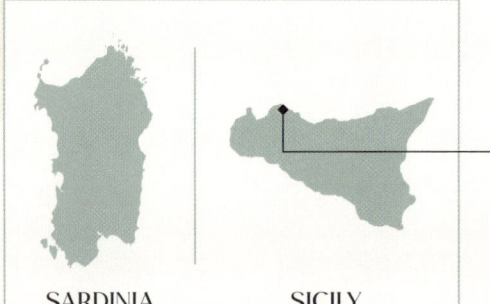

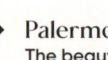

SARDINIA   SICILY

Palermo

The beautiful, troubled Sicilian capital is a synthesis of Arabic, Norman, and Spanish Baroque influences so beguiling that it's hard to understand what came from where and how. The net result is a place that challenges your ideas of what Europe is and was. There's nowhere quite like it.

Venice

The Most Serene Republic of Venice ruled the Adriatic and parts of the Aegean for over 1,000 years, turning its melancholy lagoon into a global power. Perhaps the apogee of this supremacy was Venice itself—arguably the most beautiful city ever built.

Bologna

The capital of Emilia-Romagna is nicknamed *la dotta* (the learned) for its university, the oldest in Europe; *la rossa* (the red) for both the color of its buildings and its political leanings; and *la grassa* (the fat) for its gluttonous cuisine, heavy on pastas, cured meats, and cheeses.

Naples

Famed for its hyper-Baroque architecture and the looming presence of Vesuvius, Italy's third-biggest city is an exhilarating and often incomprehensible place, one which is better felt than understood. Everyone has an opinion on Naples, though perhaps Goethe put it most succinctly: "See Naples and then die."

Rome

The Eternal City is where everyone from the Romans to the Fascists came and left their mark. Overwhelmingly beautiful, deftly rich, and frequently chaotic, Italy's capital is also the country in its purest, most essential form.

ANCIENT SITES

Unearthing the history of one of the world's greatest empires

It might be a little over 1,500 years since the last days of Rome, but we're still thinking of the Roman Empire. And who can blame us, given this gargantuan civilization shaped everything from contemporary governance to our favorite comfort food? Across the country, ancient Rome's awe-inspiring legacy remains tantalizingly alive: towering temples and echoing ruins speak eloquently of our ancient forebears, weaving a tale of genius architects, ambitious emperors, and lusty citizens.

Before the Romans

We all know Rome wasn't built in a day, but we might forget that the empire wasn't built solely by ingenious Romans, either. Before Rome's first rulers came the Greeks, who shaped Italy in their own image.

Venture to the country's south and you'll stumble upon sites a good deal older than Rome: Greek ruins. For the Greeks, expanding westward and constructing temples to the gods was an ancient rite of passage; each new territory was one step closer to forming the ideal Magna Graecia (Great Greece). Perhaps the greatest of Greek treasures is found just south of Naples, at the archaeological site of Paestum. Here lie two Temples of Hera and the Temple of Ceres, three of the world's best-preserved Greek temples. The colossal size of the Doric columns and the carved intricacy of their decoration is a living testament to Greek faith: the temples were designed as ritual spaces where gifts were left to a panoply of gods.

After centuries of peace, a swift upset came in the form of the

---

Roma non fu fatta in un giorno
Rome wasn't built in a day

Experts believe that the first reference to this well-known phrase—meaning in order to reach greatness or a goal, hard work, effort and time are required—dates back to the 12th century. The phrase was even uttered by Queen Elizabeth I in a 1563 speech, and it is still used today.

territory-hungry Romans, with Paestum conquered in 273 BCE. The Romans gradually transformed the site into a large, bustling city that would thrive for a thousand years before it was swiftly wiped out by a plague. They retained a number of the Greeks' Hellenistic features, including stone statues, open public spaces, and hefty columns. What remains—a Roman forum, amphitheater, swimming pool, grand villa, and even an early Christian church—yields fascinating insights into life in Rome's urban centers.

The fall of a city

There are few ancient centers quite as evocative as the ruined city of Pompeii in southern Italy. Hauntingly preserved under Mount Vesuvius's volcanic ash, the ruined city and the nearby towns of Herculaneum and Stabiae offer a vivid snapshot of Rome at its peak.

INSPIRED BY ITALY

Rome and Napoleon

Although he never set foot in Rome, Napoleon (1769-1821) was fascinated by the empire and idolized Rome's greatest emperors. Classic Roman architectural elements such as columns, domes, and arches were central features of his plans for a redesigned Paris.

Before the eruption of 79 CE, Pompeii, south of Naples in Campania, was a wealthy city of around 20,000 residents. This was a place of major decadence, affluence, and debauchery, the pinnacle of the ancient good life. In the summer months, wealthy Romans would arrive to let off steam: the city's brothels and erotic murals speak not of faith but of carnality and pleasure. Nestled within a crescent of fertile land—grapes, olives, tomatoes, and other crops thrived in the volcanic soil—Pompeii's affluence grew and grew. But the source of the city's success would also bring about its demise. Pompeii sat at the base of what its citizens thought was a mountain, but they knew little of the elemental power bubbling away at its core.

The volcano's infamous eruption lasted for two days. The first phase of pumice and ash rain allowed most to escape, but in the final 24 hours, there was little hope for those seeking shelter in their homes. The eruption's final wave of pyroclastic materials and gases froze people in situ. Around 2,000 Pompeiians perished, and the city—along with Herculaneum, Stabiae, and Torre Annunziata— was buried under layers of ash for centuries, never to be rebuilt.

Epic structures

Without the ash of Vesuvius, we would never have seen those fleeting details of Roman life: bodies clutching household objects, arms wrapped around loved ones. But there was no ash needed to preserve Rome's most timeless symbols. Take, for example, the mighty Colosseum, built to withstand the ravages of time. No matter how often it's been displayed on screen, this symbol of ancient Rome never fails to impress and is inevitably

♦ ♦ ♦

Previous page
Vesuvius looming
behind the ruins
of Pompeii

Above left
The House of
Neptune mosaic
at Herculaneum

Above right
The Arch of
Septimius Severus
at the Roman Forum

a must-visit for so many travelers today. Located just east of the Roman Forum in the Italian capital, the huge Colosseum was the ultimate power flex by Emperor Vespasian, who commissioned its construction in 72 CE. After the tumultuous reigns of Nero and Caligula—whose soaring egos and thirst for blood threatened to destabilize the empire—Vespasian's monumental gift to the people was seen as a powerful gesture of renewal and stability. Under his Flavian Dynasty, a mass building program sought to restore a city that had been ravaged by political despotism, fire, and ongoing civil war.

Finished in 80 CE by Vespasian's son, Titus, the Colosseum was the largest amphitheater in the world, designed to dazzle the masses with *panem et circenses* (bread and circuses). Imagine violent gladiator battles and wild animal hunts featuring lions and elephants, all with up to 80,000 spectators roaring in the stands. These epic shows continued for nearly four centuries until Emperor Honorius banned gladiatorial games in 404 CE. Historians tell of the bloody murder of a monk, Telemachus, who had attempted to stop the mindless gladiatorial bloodshed. Dismayed by the murder, Honorius swiftly closed all gladiatorial schools. Eventually, earthquakes and the Fall of Rome took their toll, leaving the Colosseum partially in ruins.

While the Colosseum was all about spectacle, the Pantheon, another epic structure, was built for worship and reflection. Meaning "all gods" in Greek (the Greek language became a favorite of the educated elite in Rome), the Pantheon was originally a temple dedicated to Roman gods.

The specific rituals and functions conducted behind its 2,000-year-old bronze doors remain a compelling mystery, however, with a host of theories about the building's many uses during its long life. The Pantheon is one of the best preserved of all ancient Roman buildings, largely because it has remained in continuous use throughout its history. In 609 CE, Pope Boniface IV converted the Pantheon into a Catholic church, Basilica di Santa Maria ad Martyres; it is thanks to this conversion that the building stands today (except for some of the missing original bronze ceiling). Following its conversion, it became the final resting place for decorated figures of high society, including Renaissance painter Raphael and King Victor Emmanuel II, the first king of united Italy.

Grand villas

The ancient Romans might have been a pious bunch, but their religious architecture was rivaled by their taste for luxury. Across Italy, ancient villas commissioned by powerful nobles give us a taste of the finer things. Villa dei Quintili, located on Via Appia Antica (the Appian Way, the world's oldest surviving road), was the grandest villa and thermal bath complex in Rome during its time. The villa was home to the noble brothers Sesto Quintilio

Condiano and Sesto Quintilio Valerio Massimo until they were executed by Emperor Commodus in 182–183 CE. And in an appropriately Roman finale, the emperor seized the villa and lived there until his death, adding to speculation that he murdered the brothers simply to snatch the property for himself. When it was excavated, it was thought to have been a town due to its large size, rather than a villa.

Then there's Villa Hadrian, a magnificent 30-building estate in Tivoli, a short way from Rome. The well-traveled emperor named areas after places he visited, including the Canopus named after the ancient Egyptian town; the building included bathhouses, huge libraries, and a couple of theaters. A fondness for opulence? Just one more thing Italy owes to its ancient ancestors.

◆ ◆ ◆

Below The dome of Rome's Pantheon with its circle hole, known as the oculus

DARIUS ARYA

◆

On the limitless wonders of Italian archaeology

Darius Arya is an archaeologist, public historian, author, and TV presenter based in Rome. He has undertaken excavations around the world, but his primary focus and key area of interest has always been the Roman Empire. We might all be thinking about the Romans, but few of us have devoted our lives to discovering their secrets quite like Arya. As part of his investigations, he has led or co-directed excavations at the Roman Forum and at Villa delle Vignacce in the Park of the Aqueducts, as well as several projects in Rome's mysterious port city, Ostia Antica.

"From the moment I first picked up a book on Greek mythology, I was hooked on the stories of gods and heroes and monsters," he says. "Archaeology allows us to learn more about our collective past, our successes, and our failures." What is it about Roman archaeology in particular that interests him? "Archaeology in Italy is unique for two reasons. One, the eruption of Vesuvius preserved a series of cities—Pompeii, Herculaneum, and Stabiae—and other related sites on a scale that is unmatched anywhere else in the world." Thanks to the ash of Vesuvius, archaeologists have been able to uncover the varied trappings of Roman life, from the grand to

the banal: "Roads, public monuments, graffiti, frescoes, wooden roofing, and objects from daily life, as well as artwork and lead pipe systems— these are truly stunning and offer insights unlike any other archaeological sites." Arya is as excited by the smallest things—"carbonized loaves of bread, seeds, wine"—as he is by the grandest buildings. It's in these everyday details that we find the traces of ancient life, after all.

And the other reason for his love of Rome? "As the capital of a sprawling empire, Rome just has *more* than any other city, due to its huge wealth for so many years. The city of Rome today is one giant museum, with unrivaled sites, monuments, and museum collections. Italy was the empire's richest province by far, so the country itself is filled with more sites and art than any other part of the ancient empire." Part of the archaeologist's job is to carefully preserve these sites, under- taking delicate conservation processes to ensure they live to see the coming decades. But the best thing for devoted archaeologists like Arya is the wealth of Roman treasures that remain to be explored. "Excavations are endless," he says. "There will always be new sites and new surprises to uncover."

◆ ◆ ◆

Clockwise from left Temple at Paestum; the Pantheon; the Colosseum; pots at Pompeii

EARLY ART

The visual culture of the ancient world

Over thousands of years, Italy's pioneering artists have changed the way we depict our world. In ancient Rome, decorative artwork was found everywhere, from temples to toilets. The Romans worked wonders with stone and plaster, creating luminous visions not only of rulers and gods but also of the humdrum details of life, love, sex, and food. Their medieval descendants inherited this rich legacy, imbuing their work with the grandeur of their early Christian faith.

Ancient images

Italy's artistry begins in antiquity, when Roman artists strove not only to emulate but to better the Hellenistic art of their Greek predecessors. A good deal of Roman public art involved sculpting powerful rulers with striking physical accuracy, with stone busts of ancestors and emperors gazing sternly from buildings both public and private.

One of the reasons we feel such familiarity with ancient Rome is that theirs was a distinctly visual culture, with artwork used to advertise and communicate as well as to challenge and inspire. A walk through Pompeii gives us a slice of daily life: meticulous and colorful paintings decorating the Villa of the Mysteries depict Dionysian rituals and cult worship. The risqué Lupanar Frescoes, found in a brothel, advertise service, while frescoes outside ancient bakeries depict the Romans' favorite dough-based goods.

Roman interiors were often lavishly painted and stuccoed, with walls depicting mythological scenes and bucolic landscapes. Many of these pieces show scenes from Greek myth, including the Sacrifice of Iphigenia, in which Agamemnon's daughter, Iphigenia, is sacrificed to appease the gods. A knowledge of Greek culture and storytelling was seen as the height of sophistication, so wealthier villas proudly displayed scenes such as these.

The method used by ancient fresco painters ensured these pieces had remarkably vivid colors, and many miraculously retain their luster to this day, almost as if the ancient artist's

POMPEII PIZZA

In 2023, a fresco of a flat, dough-based dish that looks a lot like the modern pizza was unearthed during excavations in Pompeii. The work of art is thought to depict an array of dishes that date back to ancient Greece.

brush had just left the surface. First, a thin layer of limestone plaster, known as *intonaco*, was spread over the face of the wall and then painted on while the plaster remained damp. This allowed the pigments to mix with the *intonaco* and, once it dried, the paint to be sealed into the wall. These works, many of which survive, are like stepping stones to the distant past, revealing the preoccupations and desires of the ancients better than any Hollywood dramatization ever could.

Medieval marvels

With the fall of the Roman Empire and the rise of Christianity, art shifted its attention to the Bible, with paintings depicting religious figures. Italian artists of the 11th century focused their attention on a new religious style: the altarpiece. Wooden church altars became the canvas for some of the finest works of the period, including Duccio di Buoninsegna's *The Nativity with the Prophets Isaiah and Ezekiel*, painted on a single panel of poplar. The piece was proudly displayed at Siena Cathedral for over 450 years, and Duccio di Buoninsegna became known as the father of the "Sienese school" of religious painting, a movement defined by rich, decorative colors and a vivid, dreamlike quality. Altarpiece painters turned for inspiration to the Christian East, adapting the techniques and styles of Byzantine iconography.

But fresco painting hadn't fallen entirely out of favor. In the late 13th century, Italy's most renowned painters, including Cimabue and Giotto, decorated the Basilica of St. Francis in Assisi with magnificent frescoes. Among these, Giotto's iconic cycle depicting the life of St. Francis has become the focus of Catholic pilgrimages. Giotto would continue his work in the Scrovegni Chapel in Padua, where he illustrated scenes from the lives of Christ and the Virgin Mary. His vivid colors and surrealist imagery heralded the transition from Byzantine to Renaissance art.

◆ ◆ ◆

Below left Fresco in Casa degli Amini Dorati, Pompeii
Below right Girolamo di Benvenuto's Sienese altarpiece

ITALIAN MYTHOLOGY

The legends and lore that shaped Italy

Italians are natural-born storytellers, weaving tales that have traveled through generations since the very beginning of Rome. Twin babies raised by a she-wolf, Cyclopes hiding under mountains and a witch who brings gifts to children on Epiphany Eve— it's these epic ancient tales of gods and goddesses, heroes and beasts, that continue to fire up our imaginations even today.

All roads lead to Rome

When it comes to Italy's storybook, there's hardly a grander tale in its pages than that of Rome's founding myth. Though some like to say it all began with an epic brotherly fight, Rome would not be Rome without the fall of Troy, tells Virgil in his epic *The Aeneid*, a 12-volume tale chronicling a journey that would lead to the eventual birth of Rome. After the fall of Troy, hero Aeneas escaped the burning city in Asia Minor and fled to the Italian peninsula. Centuries later, his descendants—two babies—were left abandoned in the Tiber River. Found by a she-wolf who raised them as her own, twins Romulus and Remus grew up in the surrounding hill community, and created a city in its fertile valley. But brothers will be brothers, and

Romulus killed Remus in a boundary dispute, cementing himself as the first king of Rome. Virgil's work, commissioned at the end of the 1st century BCE, aimed to connect Rome's imperial destiny to divine prophecy. Now renowned as Rome's foremost chronicler, Virgil's tales continue to be told and retold around the world.

Thanks to the Etruscans…

While we have the Romans to thank for a lot of Italy's greatest stories, they actually took inspiration from their neighbors for some of their most revered tales and belief systems. Take the Etruscans, an influential Italic people who preceded free Romans in central Italy and significantly shaped Roman practices with distinct mythological and religious traditions. One of their legendary figures, the prophet Tages, is credited with introducing key divinatory practices to the Romans, such as interpreting animal entrails and the omens of thunder and lightning, work undertaken by seers known as haruspices. As Etruscan culture was assimilated into the Roman Republic, these seers became integral to Roman society, playing vital roles by advising political leaders, participating in

◆ ◆ ◆

Previous page Statue
of Romulus and
Remus, the brothers
who founded Rome
Clockwise from right
Olympians guarding
Praetorian Fountain
in Palermo; Italy's
kind witch, La Befana;
a fresco of Cupid,
Venus, and Mars
at Pompeii

"It wasn't only
the ancients who
told riveting tales
to better understand
their world."

public ceremonies and averting negative omens.

...and the Greeks

Roman society was also centered around a polytheistic outlook, with citizens worshipping a variety of deities. One look at Rome's lineup of gods—Diana, Jupiter, Venus, Neptune—and it's easy to note the overlap with the Greek deities of Mount Olympus. Many Greek myths, including parts of Odysseus's wanderings, took place in what is now Italy, inspiring the Romans to adapt these legendary tales. Though Hellenic culture profoundly influenced ancient Rome, this blend produced a uniquely Roman pantheon.

Travel through Italy, and you'll hear these tales told in relation to the country's landscapes. Cyclopes is concealed by the ever-active Mount Etna, the witch Circe is said to dwell on the Lazio coast at Circeo, and the monster Scylla dominates the Straits of Messina. Italian children grow up immersed in these myths, learning them in school and studying sections of the *Aeneid, Iliad,* and *Odyssey.* And these myths are woven into everyday conversation. Take, for example, the expression *"Eessere tra Scilla e Cariddi,"* meaning to be stuck between a rock and a hard place—just like Odysseus, caught between the monsters Scylla and Charybdis.

Rural folktales

It wasn't only the ancients who told riveting tales to better understand their world (and to dramatize the everyday). Through the ages, rural communities across Italy nourished their lives on folktales—tales that blend lore, myth, and rumors, as well as pagan and Christian heritage. Of all these tales, none is more prevalent today than that of La Befana, the benevolent witch who rides a broomstick on the evening of January 5, delivering gifts to well-behaved children and punishing the naughty. The legend of La Befana illustrates the fusion of pagan customs and Christian traditions; her role as a gift-bringer echoes the ancient Roman festival of Saturnalia and the practices associated with Strenia, the Roman goddess of New Year's gifts. The story also intertwines with the Christian narrative of the Three Wise Men; according to legend, La Befana continues her search for the Christ child to this day.

Is La Befana still delivering gifts on an ongoing quest? Was Romulus really the founder of Rome? And did Odysseus really contend with monsters like Scylla and Charybdis? Really, the answers are beside the point when the questions make for such legendary stories.

INSPIRED BY ITALY

Age-old names

Ettore, Eros, Marcella, Julia, Aurora, Diana. Spend some time at a *parco giochi* (kids' park) and you'll hear parents calling out their children's names as if they're hailing the gods. Many names across Western Europe and beyond owe a debt to the heroes and legends of ancient myth—just another example of ancient lore permeating the everyday.

GRAND ARCHITECTURE

A world of ambitious stories carved in stone

It wasn't only through myths and fables that Italians constructed their national story. The Romans perfected ancient architecture; their descendants took it to new heights, carving out a grand narrative through their physical structures, with every cloistered church and fortified castle whispering tales of power, faith, and beauty. Across the centuries, Italians have dotted their landscapes with some of the most recognizable and beautiful structures in the world.

Classic cathedrals

Among Italy's plethora of inspiring structures, it's perhaps the cathedrals that top the list in terms of sheer swoon-worthy beauty. The grander the House of God, the deeper the devotion—or so the theory goes.

Milan's Duomo, which began construction in the 14th century, is a sublime example. Designed in the Gothic style, it has a striking sculpture-covered facade and a walkable rooftop along which gargoyles leer above huge flying buttresses. The third-largest cathedral in Europe, the Duomo birthed tales that have circulated for centuries. Those monstrous heads peering from the cathedral's towers and walls? According to a local legend, the devil appeared to Gian Galeazzo Visconti, the aristocrat who commissioned the construction of the Duomo, and ordered him to build a church filled with diabolical images.

Then there's Florence's Duomo, an embodiment of the lofty ideals of the Renaissance. The terracotta dome was the first built since Roman times, a sign of commitment to the classical grandeur of ancient Rome. Among the most recognizable features of Italy's great cathedrals, domes were associated with the heavens, their hemispherical shapes representing the fragile boundary between the physical and spiritual worlds. In Florence's case, the architects conceived of the dome, but its size and ambition exceeded the tools they had to build it. As such, the Duomo sat unfinished for 142 years, as bright minds throughout the city pondered how to erect the magnificent structure.

A land of churches

While cathedrals may take first place in terms of size and expense, Italy's religious history is also reflected in its dizzying abundance of churches—there are more than 900 in Rome alone. Churches remain an integral part of the fabric of daily life here,

Above Milan's Gothic Duomo, which took nearly six centuries to complete

whether found in the remotest hillside village or in the heart of the capital.

Ravenna is home to glorious Byzantine churches, including the Basilica of Sant'Apollinare in Classe, which glitters with 5th-century mosaics. Ravenna was the last capital of the Western Roman Empire, and its churches yield remarkable insights into the styles of Late Antiquity, when the world of the Romans was slowly dominated by the new forces of Christianity. The church's cavernous, columned interior dazzles with

◆◆◆◆◆◆◆◆◆◆◆◆◆◆◆◆◆◆◆◆◆

RAVENNA'S HERITAGE

Eight buildings in Ravenna, including the Basilica of San Vitale, the Mausoleum of Galla Placidia and the Neonian Baptistery, are part of a UNESCO World Heritage Site, listed as priceless examples of early Christian architecture.

◆◆◆◆◆◆◆◆◆◆◆◆◆◆◆◆◆◆◆◆◆

thousands of gold-hued details, each mosaic representing a perfect fusion between the Western and Eastern styles of the late 5th century.

But it isn't only the genius of Italy's architects that makes these churches so remarkable; nature plays a key role, too. Many of Italy's churches were built in spectacular locations. The Monte Sant'Angelo complex in Puglia spirals down the rock face to a cave where the archangel Michael is said to have appeared, while the church of San Pietro in Portovenere, Liguria, seems to erupt from the cliffside.

Seats of power

Italy's grand architectural prowess didn't apply only to God's houses, of course; the wealthiest used their own dwellings to advertise their power and riches. Until 1861, Italy was a collection of disparate states, and this led to a wealth of local palaces, each home to a powerful court. From the Doge's Palace in Venice (its pink-and-white colonnaded facade shimmering on the water) to Florence's Palazzo Pitti (the castlelike home of the Medici family), these were long the seats of power. Some tell the history of occupation: Palermo's Arab-Norman Palazzo Reale is home to the Cappella Palatina, a chapel blending Byzantine and Islamic architecture.

Castles and fortresses

Not all rulers lived in fairytale *palazzi*; with its history of rival states and invaders aplenty, Italy is dotted with defensive castles, too. Some hug the coast, offering a full view of the sea should enemy ships appear on the horizon. On the island of Ischia, off the coast of Naples, Castello Aragonese floats on a rock connected to the main island by a causeway. Such is

the strategic importance of the spot, which commands views of the entire Bay of Naples, that successive inhabitants stretching back to the ancient Parthenopeans built fortifications here.

Heading inland, the breathtaking Rocca Calascio—the highest fortification in the mighty Apennines—hovers over a mountain peak in Abruzzo. Construction started with the building of a small watchtower in the 10th century, before huge stones were arranged around the tower to ensure it remained entirely impregnable. Little did its builders know that the castle would never see any military action. Its robustness was severely tested, however, by a force greater than any marching army: a powerful earthquake in 1461 shook much of the castle to the ground.

Tall towers

And then there are towers. These might look as defensive as castles, but many were actually built with a more narcissistic motive. In the medieval period, the best way to flaunt your money was by building a tower bigger than your neighbor's. There are still traces of these medieval Manhattans, notably in Bologna, whose city center is dominated by the Garisenda and Asinelli towers.

In the Renaissance, towers got even fancier, like the delicate-arched, spiral-staircased Scala dei Contarini del Bovolo in Venice, and, of course, Pisa's Leaning Tower. The tower's unusual angle guaranteed it global fame, but aside from that it couldn't be more ordinary; bell towers (or campaniles, of which the Leaning Tower is one) are a beautiful characteristic of many Italian towns and villages.

Clockwise from left
Leaning Tower of Pisa, one of Italy's many bell towers; Venice's Bridge of Sighs; Doge's Palace, a Gothic masterpiece in Venice

THE STORY OF
The Bridge of Sighs

Bridges in Italy are rarely built solely for their utility; many are structures of immense and timeless beauty. Venice is home to some of the world's most wonderful bridges, with over 400 of them stretching across its labyrinth of waterways, each shrouded in legend. But it's the haunting Bridge of Sighs that captures the imagination. The ornate limestone bridge, built in around 1600 by architect Antonio Contino, was used to deliver prisoners to the Doge's Palace, where they'd be dealt their sentence. The passageway was named for the sighs of the prisoners walking over it. A brighter legend states that if a couple share a kiss while passing in a gondola, they will be granted eternal love.

UNESCO SITES

If anything reflects Italy's deep commitment to preserving its history, it's the 60 UNESCO World Heritage Sites it has to its name. This is more than any other country on Earth and goes to show just how significant its architecture, archaeological sites, and natural wonders are, all of which have been carefully preserved over the centuries to ensure they withstand the test of time. From famous natural wonders like Mount Etna to incredible archaeological sites like Agrigento, these spots are a roll call of some of Europe's most prized places; here are just a few stars topping the list.

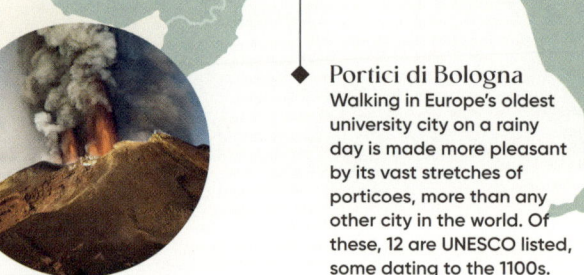

Portici di Bologna
Walking in Europe's oldest university city on a rainy day is made more pleasant by its vast stretches of porticoes, more than any other city in the world. Of these, 12 are UNESCO listed, some dating to the 1100s.

Mount Etna
On a clear day, Europe's highest and most active volcano is visible for a whopping 155 miles (250 km). Commonly referred to as "she," *bella* Etna often paints the Catania Valley with a zigzag of red lava and, rarely, smoke rings.

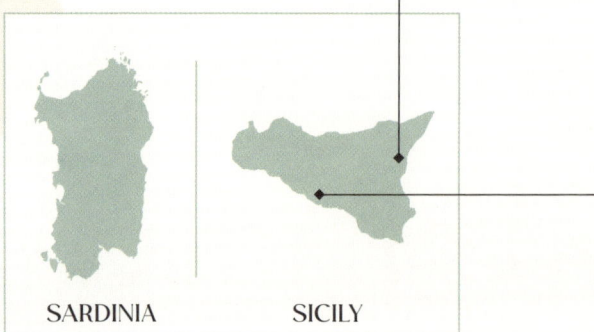

Archaeological Area of Agrigento
Formerly Akragas, Agrigento was one of the most important ancient Greek cities, founded in the 6th century BCE. Today, this area, better known as the Valley of the Temples, is dominated by the preserved remains of Doric temples.

SARDINIA   SICILY

Padua's 14th-century fresco cycles

In the 14th century, six painters decorated eight religious sites in the city of Padua, kicking off a mural revolution. At the forefront of this movement was Giotto, a painter and architect who completed the famed Scrovegni Chapel frescoes in 1305.

Trulli of Alberobello

Alberobello might seem like a whimsical gnomesville, but the 1,000 or so cone-roofed limestone *trulli* served a purpose in the mid-14th century. Legend says the ancient mortarless homes could quickly transform into rubble by pulling out the pinnacle in their roofs, an ingenious way for farmers to evade property taxes.

Via Appia Antica

Rome's 2,300-year-old *autostrada* (highway) was engineered to link Rome with Brindisi in the south and an expanding Empire. Today, a 336-mile (540 km) stretch includes a public park for walkers, cyclists, and occasional herds of goats.

Matera

An extraordinary city, Matera is fused to a cave-ridden outcrop above a deep ravine. People lived in Matera's *sassi* (caves) from the Paleolithic period until the 1950s, and the intact network of cave dwellings, churches, and houses form an astonishing maze.

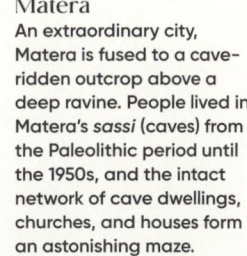

Reggia di Caserta

Built for Charles III in the 18th century, the world's largest former royal residence knows how to make a statement. Over 1,000 richly decorated rooms look out to vast gardens, where the 1.8-mile (3 km) Via d'Acqua (water street) is a particular highlight.

THE RENAISSANCE

Rebirth. That's the literal meaning of the *Rinascimento*, or Renaissance, an intellectual and cultural movement that changed the course of the Western world. And it didn't begin on a battlefield or in a hallowed royal hall—it all started in a humble Italian library.

In the mid-14th century, the scholar Petrarch was browsing rows of dusty tomes when he made a curious discovery. A lost manuscript contained the letters of the ancient Roman writer Cicero, within which the great statesman explained his boundless humanist vision of the world, one governed by rationality, artistic inquiry, and scientific interrogation, with no room for superstition or religious dogma. His thinking, which Petrarch and other Italian writers would revitalize, ignited an intellectual explosion.

Emerging from the Middle Ages, the Renaissance could not have succeeded without Italy's seemingly limitless wealth. Powerful families like the Medicis *(p202)*—rulers of Florence, the cradle of the Renaissance—threw money at artists to produce sublime works. As published works proliferated with the invention of the printing press in the mid-15th century, an increasingly literate public sought out texts from the ancient Greek and Roman worlds. Learning in all its forms was glorified, paving the way for some of the greatest thinkers and artists the world has ever known, Leonardo da Vinci, Dante Alighieri, and Machiavelli among them. The so-called "Dark Ages" were well and truly over, and the intellects of Europe were ablaze.

"It didn't begin on a battlefield or in a hallowed royal hall—it all started in a humble Italian library."

Left Pietro Perugino's Renaissance masterpiece *Delivery of the Keys*

SCIENCE AND THOUGHT

How the Renaissance created the modern mind

Italy has fostered a long tradition of scientific thought. It wasn't until the Renaissance, however, that scientific and philosophical inquiry became central to Italy's intellectual culture, with scholars rediscovering classical thinking and skills and pushing them forward. From the ability to reproduce perspective in painting and design to philosophy that challenged the idea of an omnipotent god, the Renaissance steered Europe toward modern society in more ways than imaginable.

Philosophical rebirth

First, Italy rebooted philosophy. In 1462, Medici family patriarch Cosimo de' Medici opened a school of Neo-Platonic thought, a reinterpretation of the ideas of ancient Greek philosopher Plato, which used love and the search for the infinite as a way to reach perfection. Alongside this return to the thought of Plato, there was a new strain of Humanism, an intellectual movement that looked to the classical world, led by the so-called "Father of Humanism," Petrarch. Florence was a haven for freethinkers and those who were persecuted by the Church, and Florentine voices soon became thought leaders across Europe, spreading the ideas of Humanism and Neo-Platonism across the continent. Their emphasis on humanity's power, rather than god and destiny, paved the way for the separation of Church and State.

Scientific advancement

Within this new culture of intellectual inquiry, everything was there to be questioned, including the creation of the earth and its place within the universe. Revolutionary astronomers like Galileo Galilei challenged the Church's doctrines on the cosmos, questioning the role played by an omnipotent god. For these thinkers, proof was everything, and if the rigorous methods of science couldn't validate a belief, it was dismissed as blind assumption. This thinking drew the ire of the Church, and Galileo was confined to house arrest, with many of his works banned for centuries. Scientists forged on in spite of the Church's hard line, observing and experimenting to draw their own conclusions. Astronomers realized that the earth revolved around the sun (and not the other way around); Galileo worked out a new theory of gravity (with the help of the Leaning Tower of Pisa); doctors studied anatomy to understand how bodies worked; and

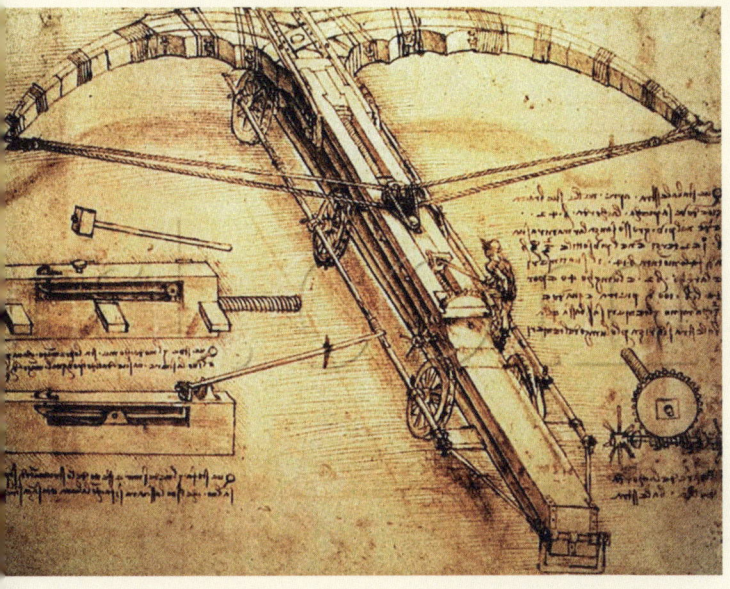

◆◆◆◆◆◆◆◆◆◆◆◆◆◆◆◆◆◆◆◆◆◆◆◆◆◆

THE STORY OF
Leonardo da Vinci

Born in the Tuscan countryside in 1452, Leonardo da Vinci was an insatiable polymath, someone who could as easily design battlements and cannon-resistant walls as he could paint a world-famous picture. He might have been the archetypal Renaissance man, but little about his own philosophy and belief system is known. He left thousands of pages of writings and drawings but said little about his personal life or thinking, fueling centuries of speculation about the life of the man himself.

◆◆◆◆◆◆◆◆◆◆◆◆◆◆◆◆◆◆◆◆◆◆◆◆◆◆

mathematicians made grand new discoveries in algebra, calculus, and geometry. The latter was used to stunning effect in the rediscovery of perspective, not only making art more lifelike but also revolutionizing architecture and public spaces.

New technologies

Alongside these new styles of architecture came new technology— an industrial revolution, as it were. Leonardo da Vinci may be best known for his art, but back in his day, he was a polymath in high demand. He left behind thousands of sketches for proposed inventions, his ravenous mind inventing flying machines and self-propelled carts. With new scientific methods and a lively spirit of inquiry, a whole world of inventions became possible— all thanks to the Renaissance.

◆◆◆

Above Leonardo's ink-drawn sketches
Right The *Lucan portrait of Leonardo da Vinci,* believed to be a self-portrait

ARTISTIC MASTERPIECES

Italy's unrivaled artistic legacy

David and *Mona Lisa*. Michelangelo and Leonardo. What other country has produced artworks and artists so iconic that they roll off the tongue? Art has always been at the heart of Italy's DNA, but it wasn't until the Renaissance that creatives took things up a notch. Artists from this time and through the Baroque period transformed the artistic landscape with innovative techniques and visionary approaches, leaving a legacy of beloved works that still attract huge lines at Italy's best galleries.

Renaissance art

The Renaissance wasn't just a rebirth—it was a revolution. Not only did it reintroduce and refine art techniques that had been lost since antiquity, it also ushered in fresh artistic methods, redefining what the world knew about art. One of the most significant advancements was the rediscovery of linear perspective. Artist Filippo Brunelleschi's groundbreaking work in perspective and architectural design—notably Florence's Duomo—led to new ways of thinking about space in public buildings. Leon Battista Alberti, architect of the facade of Florence's Santa Maria Novella, further developed ideas of perception in his treatise *Della Pittura* (1453). Little by little, artists began to adopt these new principles into their work: they created the illusion of distance by using straight lines to represent the horizon, before fixing a vanishing point to convey depth. Two-dimensional works of the Middle Ages were a thing of the past.

New creators

As these techniques were developing, so too was the idea of the "Renaissance man," a person skilled in an array of disciplines, full of boundless curiosity, intelligence, and creativity. It helped,

THE STORY OF
Plautilla Nelli

A nun as well as a self-taught painter, Florence native Plautilla Nelli (1524–1588) is considered one of the city's first female Renaissance artists. For centuries her paintings remained largely forgotten until an organization, Advancing Women Artists, rediscovered her work. One of Nelli's most impressive pieces, *The Last Supper*, was restored by the group and exhibited in the Santa Maria Novella Museum.

INSPIRED BY ITALY

Use Your Illusion

In 1991, Guns N' Roses debuted its double album *Use Your Illusion I & II*, and while everyone was hooked on "November Rai,n, they were also getting a tiny lesson in Renaissance art. The cover, designed by Mark Kostabi, features a reinterpretation of Raphael's 1511 masterpiece, *The School of Athens*, the archetypal Renaissance fresco featuring antiquity's greatest philosophers and scholars. With a bit of rock-and-roll humor, Kostabi depicts one of the secondary figures in bold colors.

♦♦♦

Previous page
The incredible ceiling of the Sistine Chapel
Clockwise from top left Michelangelo's *David*; Jesus at the center of Leonardo's *The Last Supper*; the infamous coy smile of the *Mona Lisa*

art world some of its most enduring treasures. When he wasn't drawing up complex models and scientific diagrams, polymath Leonardo da Vinci was pushing the boundaries of artistic inquiry in masterpieces like *The Last Supper* (c. 1495–1498) and the *Mona Lisa* (c. 1503–1506). His use of depth, perspective and religious symbolism is just as important as his pioneering adoption of a new technique called *sfumato*, the subtle blending of colors on the canvas to give a sense of vitality and life.

Michelangelo's approach to anatomy and emotion set new standards in art, too. He cemented his legacy with the masterful statue *David* (1504), the quintessential example of Renaissance sculpture, defined by its subject's intense focus and idealized physique. The artist would then capture the world's attention with the frescoes of the Sistine Chapel ceiling (1508–1512), namely with the painting *David and Goliath* (1509).

Following the Renaissance

While the artistic ceiling had been well and truly shattered (not to mention delectably painted), innovation didn't end with the Renaissance. If the Renaissance was all about classical realism and rational thought, the Baroque was about letting a sense of heightened emotion back in. Drama and grandeur defined the movement, spearheaded by innovative artists like Caravaggio and Gian Lorenzo Bernini. A genius of sculpture and architecture, Bernini's flair for intense movement, expression, and emotion pervade all of his major sculptures, including the unforgettable *Ecstasy of St. Teresa* (1647–1652), defined by its theatrical and lifelike sense of motion and feeling.

of course, that wealthy cardinals, merchants, and aristocrats—notably the Medici family *(p202)*—provided these men (and they were always men) with the resources to explore their innovative ideas. No longer burdened by financial struggles, they were able to dedicate their time to painting, sculpture, and architecture. The results were trailblazing, producing color, perspective, and anatomical accuracy the world had never seen before. This combination of new and rediscovered techniques laid the groundwork for Western art as we know it, leaving behind a cornucopia of masterpieces.

The epitome of the "Renaissance man," artists produced scores of groundbreaking paintings, giving the

◆◆◆

Left Artemisia
Gentileschi's
*Judith Slaying
Holofernes,* a
vivid depiction
of violence

Caravaggio, meanwhile, set aside playfulness in favor of intense, dramatic scenes that achieve a nearly photographic realism. This is down to his masterful use of chiaroscuro, a technique employing stark contrasts between light and dark to create the illusion of depth on a flat surface, as seen in great works like *The Martyrdom of St. Matthew* (1599–1600). It's a style that continued in the following decades with artists like Artemisia Gentileschi, whose bloodthirsty *Judith Slaying Holofernes* (c. 1612–1613) showcased dramatic storytelling and striking technique.

The response to such extravagance was a return to simplicity and a revival of classical ideals. The Enlightenment, a cultural movement that spanned the 17th and 18th centuries, brought about a heightened interest in the classics, thanks, in part, to the rediscovery of Pompeii. Neo-Classical and Romantic artists like Antonio Canova took renewed inspiration from ancient Greece and Rome, with Canova's sculptures depicting classic Greek scenes. These artists continued to refine their style as the artistic scene evolved, but the Renaissance remains Italy's most cherished artistic era.

VALERIA MERLINI AND DANIELA STORTI

On restoring and conserving Italy's artistic treasures

"Timeless" is an adjective we often apply to great works of Italian art, as though their beauty will last forever. But as much as we'd like to think the masterpieces of Michelangelo and Caravaggio will exist indefinitely, paintings aren't immune to the ravages of time. So who's keeping these wonders in perfect shape?

Since forming their professional partnership in 1989, Valeria Merlini and Daniela Storti have restored some of Italy's greatest paintings at the esteemed Merlini-Storti Art Restoration Studio in Rome. "During our career we've had the privilege of working on many master-pieces," says Merlini. "Among these it's worth mentioning three paintings by Caravaggio: the *Madonna of the Pilgrims* (1604), the first version of the *Conversion of Saul* (1600), and the *Adoration of the Shepherds* (1609)." Working on these has been the highlight of their career, but each project came with difficulties: "The *Madonna of the Pilgrims* was a very challenging restoration, considering the importance of the painting and the responsibility you feel in putting your hands on such a precious canvas."

Ironically, perhaps, the sign of a successful art restorer is that they leave little trace of their work, as if the painting had been touched by no hand other than its creator's. But how is such a feat achieved? "First of all, it's fundamental to deeply understand the work of art you have to restore. There must be a technical and stylistic understanding of the artwork." These skills are practical, too: "Having knowledge of chemistry is fundamental as we deal with solvents, varnishes, and similar materials every day." And, perhaps most importantly, the restorer must suppress her own creative preferences: "A restorer has to be humble and sensitive towards the artwork and its originality, putting aside any whim of creativity and making sure the center of the restoration is following the lead of the artist."

Looking ahead, Merlini and Storti hope to raise awareness of the vital importance of art restoration. "Making the work of restorers more known is very important. The reason why anyone can go to a museum and see masterpieces from the 15th, 16th, 17th centuries–or earlier–in perfect condition is because we have restorers taking care of them." It's a welcome reminder that next time we gaze on a Caravaggio or Leonardo, we should spare a thought for the hands who keep these pieces alive.

CARAVAGGIO'S FINAL YEARS

If there was an original bad boy of Italian art, it would be Caravaggio. Born Michelangelo Merisi da Caravaggio in 1571, the artist enjoyed a 14-year career in Rome that brought him more enemies than fans. When his paintings were first unveiled, they were controversial to say the least, featuring unorthodox composition, expressive emotions, and dramatic and often violent realism. Not that this sense of scandal put people off; despite being criticized publicly, his work was coveted, collected, and even copied.

But what of his personal life? A prolific brawler, Caravaggio repeatedly upset the wrong people. By 1606, he was on the run from Rome, having mortally wounded a man in the city, allegedly fighting over a tennis match or a woman (there's always more than one story where Caravaggio is concerned). For the next four years, he sought refuge around the Mediterranean, but his violent temperament persisted. While in Malta, he assaulted a knight before fleeing to Naples, where he continued to paint on the run. His last work, *The Martyrdom of St. Ursula* (1610), was a self-portrait in which the artist himself bears witness to a violent murder. Shortly after this was painted, Caravaggio mysteriously died while heading back to Rome.

Rumors circulated immediately and have lasted to this day, with art detectives scouring his work for clues. Assassination by one of his many enemies? Lead poisoning? Syphilis? No one knows. Caravaggio was always fond of mystery, and his unexplained death was his final and most perplexing enigma.

> "A prolific brawler, Caravaggio repeatedly upset the wrong people."

Left Caravaggio's final work, *The Martyrdom of St. Ursula*

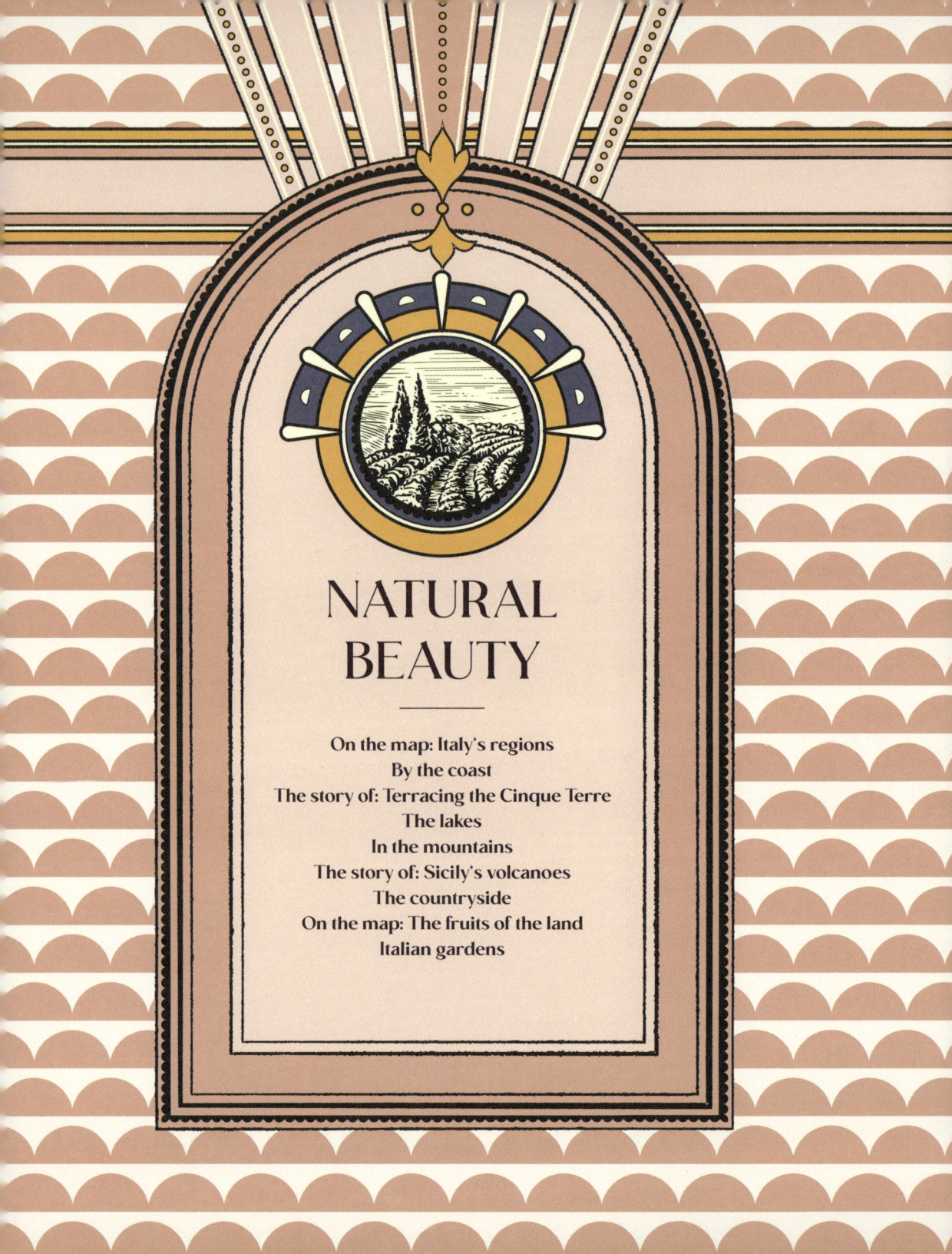

NATURAL BEAUTY

There's no two ways about it: Italy is a stunner. One of the main reasons we book holidays here is to be swept up in its incredible beauty—to drive through the fertile valleys of Tuscany, ski down the snowcapped peaks of the Alps, and stroll some of Europe's best gardens. But all that beauty isn't just for show; Italy's landscape has helped build this nation. Because if the beautiful boot didn't have a coastline, trade may not have been so abundant, and the Romans wouldn't have found this land so fruitful. Without the country's agricultural bounty, Italian cuisine and wine may not have become as popular as they are today. And if Italy's mountains and lakes didn't have such soul-stirring beauty, local poets wouldn't have felt so inspired (and we wouldn't have such great reading material). Change any aspect of the geography and Italy's story could've been very different. Fortunately, it wasn't—and that's something to be grateful for when you're exploring this beautiful country.

ITALY'S REGIONS

Italy's 20 regions are so different that traveling between them can feel like changing countries, continents, and even time periods. The peninsula's incredible diversity was influenced as much by its rugged landscape as by its history of warring empires and rival states. With such startling variety, it's no wonder that Italians still refer to their country as *il bel casino*, the beautiful mess.

Liguria

Comprised almost entirely of mountains plunging directly into the sea—with flat land at a premium—Liguria's landscape forced its residents to get creative. Today, their terraced vineyards and villages still seem to defy explanation.

Sardinia

An island adrift in the Mediterranean Sea, Sardinia is an otherworldly landscape of Caribbean-esque beaches and rugged mountains. It's not only geographically apart from the mainland; numerous dialects and languages are still spoken here.

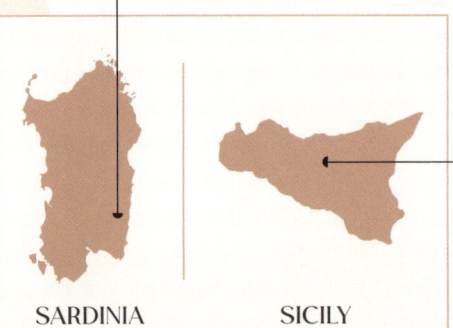

SARDINIA   SICILY

Sicily

Endless empires have been and gone from the island's shores, but Sicily remains. A cornucopia of culture, this volcanic island is famous for the Baroque cities of the Val di Noto, the Greek temples of the south coast and the perilous villages around the rumbling Mount Etna.

Veneto

The flat, marshy islands of the lagoon dominate popular images of Veneto, but this region also takes in the shores of Lake Garda, the hills of Valdobbiadene and a large slice of the Alps, including the dreamscapes of Cortina.

Trentino-Alto Adige

Three languages, two provinces, and one astonishing landscape: that's Trentino-Alto Adige. The rooftop of Italy is entirely sequestered in the Alps and is home to its most impressive natural monuments. Every valley, every village, and every vista feels like it came straight from a dream.

Abruzzo

Rugged mountain landscapes rule in the sparsely populated region of Abruzzo. Here, national parks and Apennine mountains form a wild and pristine paradise, occasionally interrupted by isolated hill towns where time seems to move slowly. It's a region that's almost impossible to finish exploring.

Tuscany

This is a region so famous that it's effectively a brand unto itself. Tuscany is home to an Elysian landscape of rolling hills, trickling rivers, and winding lanes watched over by cypress trees, offering nourishment for the soul.

Puglia

The stiletto on Italy's boot, Puglia's flat and seamless landscape encompasses endless olive groves, sugar-cube houses—known as *trulli*—and a coastline of arid dunes and towering, forested cliffs.

BY THE COAST

Life surrounded by the Mediterranean Sea

A peninsula surrounded on three sides by the shimmering Mediterranean, Italy is a country proudly defined by its coasts. The approximately 4,600 miles (7,500 km) of shoreline are home to every imaginable seascape. Flat stretches of foreshore and great sandy beaches dominate to the east along the wild Adriatic. To the northwest, the Ligurian Sea meets a jagged arc of rocky promontories and clifftop villages, the pastel-painted Cinque Terre foremost among them. Perhaps the most beloved stretch of all lies to the south, where the whitewashed homes of the Amalfi Coast perch vertiginously over the Tyrrhenian Sea. And then there are the islands—Sardinia, Sicily, and the smaller Capri, Elba, and Ischia, to name a few—where life has long been dictated by the rhythm of the seas.

Stories of the sea

This glorious abundance of coastline has meant the sea plays a key role in Italy's national story. It's little wonder that Virgil, ancient Rome's most famous poet, has been called the greatest chronicler of the seas: the ocean features heavily in his work, and the *Aeneid* shows a deep intimacy with the Mediterranean, as his characters crest its waves in great ships or perish in the sea's mightiest storms.

For centuries after Virgil, the oceans were Italy's means of exploring the world. Crossing the sea's mighty expanse was essential for maritime republics to expand their influence. Pioneering Venetian navigators like Marco Polo sent their vessels out across the Adriatic, bringing back riches and turning Venice into Europe's wealthiest city by the 13th century. At the peak of its maritime power, Venice had 36,000 sailors operating 3,300 ships, and dominated the seas.

From exploration to vacation

Today, of course, the Italian coast is associated less with sea-loving poets

PORTOFINO'S PAINTED HOUSES

Along the shoreline of Portofino, houses are painted in gelato pastels that depict windows, doors, and balconies, which are actually mere illusions—trompe-l'œil tricks designed to fancy up the facade of the buildings in the style of the genuine sculptures, cornices, and marbles that were used to decorate rich residences in Genoa.

THE STORY OF
La Fontelina, Capri

After World War II, beach tourism became a mass phenomenon across Italy, with newly opened luxury beach clubs attracting high-profile guests from film and TV. Few clubs were as esteemed as Capri's La Fontelina, built on a patch of coast once favored by Roman emperors. In the 1960s, the International Jet Set discovered the wonders of Capri, and La Fontelina welcome legendary guests like Brigitte Bardot, Sophia Loren, and Clark Gable. Today, the club remains a staple on the summer yacht itineraries of countless celebrities and supermodels.

"Beach clubs sustain a uniquely Italian approach to the seaside."

sun loungers and umbrellas, lined up in neat rows along the beach, and backed by a row of dainty wood-slat changing cabins. Prices are often determined, not by the beauty of the beach, but by the society that frequents the club, with many beachgoers paying a steep premium to sunbathe near soccer stars and TV personalities.

Today, there are thousands of beach clubs throughout the country. This might be to the chagrin of natural beach lovers—these clubs usually charge a fee for a day or a season—but the clubs sustain a uniquely Italian approach to the seaside that's more about sociability than wild swimming.

Plain sailing

Though many Italians now enjoy the sight of the sea from the comfort of their beach towels, some still prefer to meet the waves head on. Italy has a rich sailing culture stretching back thousands of years, with the country's rocky periphery and outlying islands luring seafarers from all over the world. Every stretch of coast is rife with tales of sailors who met their tragic ends or who returned to their pining lovers against all odds.

Few coastal sights are as glamorous as the yachts that drift lazily along the Tuscan coast between the islands of Elba, Giglio, Capraia, and Pianosa. The area is one of the most popular with

and intrepid navigators and more with beach towels, striped umbrellas, and tan lines. The Italian concept of *villeggiatura*—essentially "resting in pleasant places"—sees residents of towns and cities fleeing en masse come August and heading for the azure waters. And once they arrive at the beach, the holiday begins.

Deeply tied to notions of vacation in Italy are the beach clubs that occupy the majority of the country's swimmable shoreline. The first *stabilimenti balneari* (bathing establishments) opened in the 19th century along the Adriatic coast of Rimini and Versilia. Each beach club occupies a section of the beach, marked out by its own brightly colored

•••
Previous page
Lounging on the sands of Capri
Clockwise from top left Sardinia's Bassa Trinita beach; the shores of Portofino; a small cove on the south coast

affluent sailors who moor some of the world's most expensive yachts. The country is also home to the largest sailing regatta in the world, the Barcolana. Since its origin in 1969, the event has dominated the entire Gulf of Trieste, with almost 3,000 boats and more than 16,000 sailors. The event is the culmination of Italy's packed sailing calendar, as expert sailors and amateur enthusiasts race alongside each other.

But Italy's waters aren't only sailed by luxury yachts, of course. Fishing is deeply embedded in Italian culture, and small fishing boats are as integral to the seaside aesthetic as holiday vessels. Many of the seaside resorts we know and love started life as traditional fishing villages, and it's Italy's seasoned fisherfolk who know the country's seas better than anyone. As beautiful and beloved as it is, the Mediterranean provides livelihoods as well as picture postcards.

INSPIRED BY ITALY

Islands on screen

Film audiences got dazzling glimpses of Italy's beaches when *The Talented Mr. Ripley* and *Il Postino* hit theaters, establishing the sheer cliffside drops, colorful seaside villages, and turquoise waters of islands like Capri, Ischia, and Procida as dream destinations.

•••

Above A sailboat anchored in Paradies
Left A Sicilian fisherman with his nets

ALESSANDRO BOSCU

—●—

On sailing the beautiful coast of Italy

When Alessandro Boscu Bianchi Bandinelli sets out for the shores of Sicily or Sardinia, many islanders recognize the green hull of his yacht long before it docks. The beautiful *Santander of Wight* was designed by American naval architect Philip Rhodes in 1957, but the ship is perhaps most famous for starring as Jude Law's sloop in the 1999 film *The Talented Mr. Ripley*. The yacht has been in the Bianchi Bandinelli family for over six decades, and Alessandro Boscu has been sailing it for four of those. Few sailors can speak of the wonders of the Italian shoreline—or the pleasures of sailing with Jude Law–as passionately and knowledgeably as he can.

"I can draw the coastline from here to Sicily, I know it so well," he says from Villa di Geggiano, the vast estate in Siena that his family have called home since 1527. "Island to island, coast to coast. The south is so beautiful." Boscu has taken a brief break from picking grapes on his vineyard; he now divides his year between sailing and winemaking. For most lovers of Italian culture, such a routine sounds pretty close to paradise, and his good fortune is not lost on Boscu. "I'm doing the two things I love most in my life: making wine and sailing boats. I'm thankful to

God every single day!" That said, Boscu is all too aware of the hardships of a life at sea. For many years he has been solely responsible for the upkeep and maintenance of his ship, undertaking backbreaking tasks to keep the old vessel afloat and gleaming year after year. This labor is only getting harder as Boscu gets older, and he's often thinking of the boat's future.

A passionate sailor, Boscu recognizes that Italians have long had an intimate relationship with the sea. "Italy, as you can see from the map, is just one big dock. It has been reached by almost every population in the world–from Africa, from the east." In the Middle Ages, the Italian city–states were defined by the riches brought by maritime commerce: "There was Genoa, Amalfi, Pisa, Venezia–the four main sea republics. The sea has always been a big part of life here, and it always will be."

He pauses, just long enough for that all important question. And sailing with Jude Law? "He's a cool guy–we sailed together for two days. They filmed for a month and a half–and the boat was seen in the film for just seven minutes." It may be brief, but the *Santander of Wight* makes quite the cameo.

TERRACING THE CINQUE TERRE

Cinque Terre is never more striking than when viewed from the sea. The coastline between La Spezia and Levanto is one of the most dramatic in Liguria, its undulating cliffs and pastel houses spilling vertically into the jade water. It might first appear like this is a wild stretch of rocky cliffside, but look closer and you'll see neat terraces arranged in rows along the rocks—there are 4,450 miles (7,000 km) of these terraces in total. And that lush greenery in between each terrace? That's vine after vine, growing in abundance and plaiting each row together.

People mistakenly believe the villages that make up the Cinque Terre thrive off the sea. In fact, for centuries, the people here have lived on agriculture. The Ligurian peoples first settled these rugged clifftops, far from marauding pirates. Around 1000 CE, as the seas became safer, they started moving downward. As they did so, they terraced the sheer cliffs to make them suitable for agriculture, whittling 4,942 acres (2,000 ha) of terraces from the rock face and knitting them together with dry-stone walls (using the rocks they'd chipped off the cliff) and imported earth.

Nobody knows why they chose to master the cliffs when there was a fertile valley just on the other side of them. But their incredible legacy remains in the wine that is still produced here, against all odds. Writers Boccaccio and Dante both sang the praises of Cinque Terre's viticulture centuries ago; today, drinking the region's delicious wines helps preserve the terraces, which, themselves, stabilize those fragile cliffs.

> "Look closer and you'll see neat terraces arranged in rows along the rocks."

Left Cliffs around the Cinque Terre village of Riomaggiore

57

THE LAKES

The enduring allure of the Italian lake district

Italy may have its rivals when it comes to beautiful mountains and beaches, but few countries have lakes like these. The country's shimmering bodies of water—Como, Maggiore, and Garda, to name only the most famous—were carved out by hulking glaciers during the Pleistocene era and are dotted with historic islands and surrounded by snow-tipped peaks. They conjure up images of opulence—boat jaunts, slow lunches, palatial garden strolls—and have inspired generations of artists with their beauty (some suggest it's the beautiful Lake Como glimpsed in the background of Leonardo's *Mona Lisa*).

Lakeside luxury

Perhaps the first admirers of the lakes' beauty were the Romans. While there's evidence of prehistoric inhabitants on the shores of Lake Como, Maggiore, and Garda, it wasn't until this great civilization that the northern lakeshores began to develop, and the bodies of water became prized for their aesthetic value. Ancient writer, lawyer, and polymath Pliny the Younger had two villas on Lake Como: Villa Commedia and Villa Tragedia.

As with so many things, later generations took their cue from the Romans, bolstering Lake Como's luxury infrastructure over the centuries. Lake Como today, along with lakes Maggiore (near the border with Switzerland) and Garda (north of Verona), is known for luxury hotels and ties to Italy's aristocracy. On Como's western prong, at estates such as Villa del Balbianello and Villa d'Este, manicured gardens beckon and private boats dock for well-heeled travelers.

Restorative retreats

But the lakes aren't prized only for their beauty. Since the days of the Romans, they've also been celebrated for the health-enhancing properties of their waters. Garda, along with Orta, has long been a destination for rejuvenating the mind and the body. In Sirmione, on Garda's south shore, weary bodies dip in thermal waters at a plethora of spas and resorts, many of which date back thousands of years. Ancient Roman writer Catullus praised Sirmione as the "Pearl of Garda" as he himself took advantage of this oasis of wellness, looking out over Garda's twinkling expanse.

Art and adventure

Though they may be perfect for rest and relaxation, the lakes are also playgrounds for outdoor recreation, and they have been since the days of the Grand Tour. English Romantic poet William Wordsworth penned a good deal of verse while trekking the hills around Como, which he described as "a treasure which the Earth keeps to itself" (ironically, such words encouraged thousands to visit in his wake). The lake's trails are now frequented by countless writers, artists, and photographers seeking that same bolt of creative inspiration.

Nature seekers also head for Iseo, east of Orta, where wild swimming, smooth kayaking, and trekking to the top of a car-free island are likely high on the outdoor agenda. With a patchwork of evocatively named trails snaking around the lakeshores and up into the snowcapped mountains, it's little wonder that for every visitor arriving in stilettos, there's another in hiking boots.

●●●

Left The waters of Lake Como, Italy's third largest lake
Below The ancient town of Sirmione, on the shores of Lake Garda

THE STORY OF
Goethe in Garda

The lakes have beguiled many visiting writers over the centuries, including German writer Wolfgang Goethe. In 1786, Goethe set off on a boat trip to Malcesine, a town on the lake's eastern shore. Inspired by Malcesine's scenery, he started to sketch a castle before him—a seemingly innocent act that caused the police to believe he was a spy. What followed was an interrogation (and his sketch being torn up) until he managed to convince the authorities he was innocent. It was, naturally, recounted in his writings with both frustration and humor.

Clockwise from top
left Boats moored
at Lake Garda;
Lake Como; terrace
overlooking Como;
Loreto Island on
Lake Iseo

IN THE MOUNTAINS

The legend of Italy's geological giants

Jutting across the northernmost tip of the mainland before soaring down its central channel, Italy's mountain ranges shape the country's wild terrain. The peninsula is crisscrossed by three towering ranges—the Alps, the Dolomites, and the Apennines—whose lofty peaks and verdant valleys have long been sanctuaries of adventure and inspiration. These mountains act as rugged physical borders, separating rural communities to such a degree that one mountain village differs markedly from another, with a romantic swirl of languages and legends.

The mighty Alps

Mountainous terrain defines much of the European landscape, but one range eclipses all others in global renown: the Alps. Around 27 percent of this towering range lies in Italian territory, more than any other country bar Austria. The highest peaks are in the western Alps, including the loftiest point of all, right on the Italian-French border: Mont Blanc (or Monte Bianco as it's known to Italians). It's in these parts where you'll find hardy beasts perfectly adapted to life at higher climes. The chamois is the envy of many a mountaineer: an agile climber,

it deftly scales the higher mountain peaks at remarkable speed.

Forming a majestic part of the southern limestone Alps, but often considered a range in their own right, are the Dolomites. Even if it can't quite be articulated, the Dolomites feel different from their Alpine cousins. Their power is truly disarming, with jagged peaks and pale rocks that turn shades of pink and blue in the evening light.

The otherworldly beauty of the Dolomites has inspired a mosaic of myths. The Ladins, an ethnolinguistic group based in the mountains for millennia, shrouded their home peaks in legend by documenting their great saga, the *Kingdom of the Fanes*. Circulated since pre-Roman times, the saga tells of a legendary realm that sinks beneath the earth, its inhabitants destined to wait forever in the mountains for its return.

The spine of Italy

Then there's the Apennines, a range that pummels down the center of Italy in a flurry of fits and starts before tumbling into the sea off the coast of Calabria. The neat, orderly valleys of the Alps these are not; rather, the Apennines are a maze of mountains

THE STORY OF

Mountain languages

A history of isolation and invasion have turned Italy's mountain ranges into some of Europe's most linguistically diverse terrains. Indeed, these are the last holdouts of some of the continent's rarest languages and dialects. Two dialects, Cimbrian and Mòcheno, are found in a handful of scattered villages along the Trentino-Veneto border, forming the southernmost outposts of the German language, while many in the ski town of Courmayeur still speak the local patois, Valdôtain.

and canyons encircling cities, towns, and villages. This is also some of the country's last true wilderness. In Abruzzo, nearly half of the region is preserved as national parks that are home to packs of wolves, lynx, deer, and wild boar.

If the Apennines were to have a mystic mountain, it would be Mount Vettore, the highest peak of the Monti Sibillini, which owe their name to Sibyl—a witch, ghost, spirit, fairy, or oracle (depending on which village you ask). Legend has it that the Sibyls would descend into the villages of Umbria and Marche at night to dance with the boys and educate the girls in weaving, before disappearing by sunrise. With landscapes as sublime as the Italian Apennines, it's little wonder these mountains loom so large in Italy's national imagination.

● ● ●

Above Lago di Braies in the heart of the Italian Dolomites
Right Winter hiking near Mont Blanc

THE STORY OF

•••

SICILY'S VOLCANOES

Italy's volcanoes have birthed fiery legends of mythic proportions. And nowhere is their tectonic force more keenly felt than Sicily, which sits near the geologically volatile Aeolian archipelago. Sicily is home to a number of volcanoes, including the wonderfully named Stromboli and Vulcano, but the most famous is, of course, Mount Etna, Europe's tallest and most active volcano.

Stories of Etna's ferocity take us back to the heady world of Greek myth. According to the Greeks, the god Hephaestus was thrown from Mount Olympus after a heated altercation with Jupiter. Landing on the island of Sicily, he selected Etna as the base for his blacksmith's forge, where he would craft almighty weapons for the Olympian gods. Every fiery spark from the volcano was taken as a sign of Hephaestus working away at his almighty anvil.

These stories of fire and fury endure, but Sicilians have since developed a more benign relationship with their volcano. Etna is locally referred to as A' Muntagna (the mountain) or simply Idda (she), in reference to the motherly role Etna has long been ascribed. Etna is both a provider—the water-abundant slopes with their fertile lavic soil have made the region one of the most sought-after terrains for wine growing—and the ultimate destroyer. The stories may change, but one thing remains constant: Etna's rumblings are a ceaseless reminder that it's nature in charge here.

"Stories of Etna's ferocity take us back to the heady world of Greek myth."

Left The flanks of Etna, shrouded in mist

THE COUNTRYSIDE

Tending to roots in the rolling hills

Images of the rolling Tuscan hills have been seen on a thousand postcards and guidebook covers, their undulating flanks fringed with orchards and vineyards. This might be a characteristic image of rural Italy, but it's just one. Between the northern snowcapped peaks of the Alps and the rugged southern shores of Sicily are myriad stretches of countryside and a patchwork of rural towns. The incredible diversity of Italy's heartland has provided endless inspiration to poets and painters while fostering ways of living that have hardly changed in centuries.

Caring for the land

Agriculture and tourism are significant industries in more rural parts of the country, and have long provided livelihoods for many Italians. Puglia's flat and highly fertile land produces the largest amount of olive oil in Italy, for example, and the region's olive harvest is a period steeped in history, folklore, and tradition. Every year in November, the most intense phase of the harvest begins, with efforts continuing into December (and even January if the season has been fruitful). The winding country lanes and streets of small agricultural towns are treated to the intense scent of the first oil pressing, as farming communities come together to press their oil. The harvest is so storied and the activity so frenzied that many tourists volunteer just to soak up the unique Puglian atmosphere (often underestimating the intense effort involved).

Much farther north, in Umbria, mushrooms and truffles are prized produce for foragers who search the region's meadows and forests. At its essence, Umbrian truffle hunting remains a beautifully simple way of life: hunters roam the land with their dog, a small spade, and a leather bag to house their spoils. In rural villages, most families have had at least one truffle hunter in their midst for centuries past.

Tuscan winemakers, meanwhile, hand-pick grapes from the vines during the *vendemmia* (grape harvest), turning only the very best bunches into world-renowned bottles. The Tuscan grape harvest, while an important part of the region's tradition, has become a lucrative aspect of the tourist industry, with places like Arezzo, Radda in Chianti, Siena, Florence, and the beautiful San Gimignano running harvest tours for visitors.

THE STORY OF
Sheep in Sardinia

They might be surrounded by the sea, but Sardinians are shepherds, not fishers. They even have their own breed of sheep—the Sarda—which has been reared specifically to produce the best Pecorino, that beloved Sardinian cheese. Sardinians love their sheep, but shepherding is no longer a lucrative career for young Sardinians, and shepherds have even been brought over from Kyrgyzstan to tend the island's flocks.

Rural challenges

Keeping these agricultural traditions alive comes with a number of pressing challenges, though. For one, ever-rising temperatures mean less snowfall in the Alps, which means less spring runoff for the Po Valley, the intensively farmed breadbasket of Italy. The issue is worse in the south, where the rains aren't falling like they used to, and foreign-born diseases such as *xylella* are wreaking havoc on the famous olive groves of Puglia. There's also the problem of many farming families leaving the land in favor of stable incomes and shorter working days as factory hands in nearby towns and cities. As idyllic as Italian rural living may seem to an outsider, the work is hard and the routines are punishing, so it can be tough to find and retain reliable agricultural workers.

But Italian farmers have always managed to find creative solutions. In Puglia's case, it's training sniffer dogs in detecting *xylella*, which has already seen positive results in hindering the spread of the disease. A younger generation of farmers are pioneering sustainable approaches to the land, with organic processes protecting regional biodiversity and reducing pesticides. With such a profound connection to the country-side, Italians won't give up preserving their land and its varied traditions without a fight.

Rugged wilderness

Though much of Italy's terrain is taken up by fertile land used for growing crops, a great deal more remains wild and untamed. Italy's countryside encompasses vast stretches of wilderness: the deeper into the country you venture, ancient olive groves and rolling hillsides give way to huge swathes of green and rich biodiversity. It was Italy's first king, Victor Emmanuel II, who decided to enclose the area around the Gran Paradiso mountain in order to protect the Alpine ibex from poachers. In 1922, his grandson, Victor Emmanuel III, donated the land to the government who subsequently unveiled it as Italy's first national park. Since then, Italians' consciousness of their natural beauty has only grown.

By the outbreak of World War II, national parks had been established in Aosta Valley, Piedmont, Lombardy, Trentino-Alto Adige, Lazio, Abruzzo, and Molise. After the war, many of the country's most precious beauty spots were given national park status, too, from Vesuvius in 1991 to the dreamy La Maddalena archipelago in 1994. In 2016, Italy's newest national park was established on the Sicilian island of Pantelleria, creating a network of untouched, protected wildernesses from the Alps all the way to the glimmering islands strung far out across the southern Mediterranean. Numbering 24 today, the country's national parks couldn't be further from its cultivated valleys, but that's the very beauty of Italy's vast countryside.

Country towns

The beloved Italian countryside isn't all isolated farmland or pristine wilderness, of course. A common sight is the hill town. Dotting the landscape from north to south, with a great concentration in Tuscany and Umbria, hill towns were born as practical defensive settlements before gradually growing into centers of political, cultural, and economic autonomy. Their circular cluster of huddled houses is an urban landscape

Previous page The Val d'Orcia, a classic Tuscan landscape **Clockwise from far left** Sheep grazing in Sardinia; a farmer tending to the land; Aosta Valley in northwest Italy

of necessity transformed into a work of art. There are several standout examples: quaint towns make up much of Sicily's interior, Piedmont's wine-growing regions, and the bucolic hillsides of Emilia-Romagna. Perhaps the quintessential hill town is San Gimignano in Tuscany. San Gimignano is a fever dream devised by 13th-century aristocrats who sought to show off their power by building taller and taller towers. By the middle of the 14th century, some 70 towers dotted the skyline before the Black Death put an end to the town's fortunes. In Umbria, meanwhile, the town of Orvieto is one of the most beautiful spots in central Italy. The ingenious Etruscans—who settled Umbria and Tuscany long before the Romans—hollowed out the hillside into a series of caverns and caves. But it's the wonders atop the hill that truly mesmerize, with ancient hilltop buildings commanding fine views over Umbria's verdant plains.

●●●

Above left Olives growing in Tuscany
Above right Hill town of San Gimignano

LE SPIGHE VERDI

Despite its seemingly irresistible allure, the communities of rural Italy are suffering as young people move away to the cities. But some are taking action. Le Spighe Verdi is an annual award given to municipalities that invest in enhancing their rural heritage. By developing sustainable and inclusive practices, it's hoped that young people can be lured back to a meaningful and sustainable way of life in the countryside.

ARIANE LOTTI

On organic farming in the wild heart of Tuscany

It's rice harvest time at Tenuta San Carlo, a farm in southern Tuscany. The farm comprises more than 1,200 acres (480 hectares), much of which is protected by the wild Maremma Regional Park. Depending on the season, you might see green rice shoots or ordered rows of chickpeas set against umbrella pines and small stretches of marshland. Listen carefully, and you can hear the gentle crashing of the Mediterranean to the south. It's a remarkable scene, something not lost on the farm's manager, Ariane Lotti, who has known the land for most of her life. "I inherited this land when my grandparents passed away," she says. "I used to come to the farm during summers when I was a kid."

Lotti has studied and worked in sustainable agriculture since she was 17, and under her and her sister Samantha's careful stewardship, Tenuta San Carlo is now fully organic-certified. Lotti feels passionately about protecting Italy's precious landscapes and its long-standing agricultural traditions. "In Italy, the landscape dictates history," she explains. "A lot of Italian land is marginal, meaning it's challenging to grow crops, so the traditional systems that developed over time have always had to be innovative." This legacy of innovation is kept alive by likeminded farmers, who continue to feel a close kinship with the land. "Many Italians live a lot closer to rural areas; there's a deep connection to rural land that goes beyond food production. It's about recreation, tourism, even something as simple as taking a walk. There's a more physical connection with the landscape."

For Lotti, achieving organic certification meant adopting an entirely new system of land management. "Organic certification, if done well, is a different system of business, a whole new philosophy regarding agricultural cycles. You have to be more in tune with the land and the seasons." This onus on sustainability creates a different relationship with the land's bounty, for the consumer as for the grower. "In the fall, every weekend there's a food festival; in Italy, there's still an appreciation of where food comes from."

The process certainly hasn't been easy for Lotti—particularly dealing with Italy's "high level of bureaucracy and the larger threat of climate change"—but Tenuta San Carlo is now a pioneering example of Italy's agricultural future. As Lotti says, "organic farming provides the best practices in the face of a changing climate."

THE FRUITS OF THE LAND

As well as being beautiful, Italy's land is incredibly bountiful. But those tomatoes you know and love? They're not an indigenous fruit. Many of the notable plants that now grow in abundance across the country were imports: tomatoes from South America, basil rooted from India, rice sprouted from the Middle East. These ingredients are now central to Italy's diverse culinary palette, and though they might have originated elsewhere, they're hard to separate from local regions in Italy.

Basil, Liguria

Basilico was ornamental until the 19th century, when the first recipe for Liguria's famed *Pesto alla Genovese*—the paste of basil, pine nuts, garlic, olive oil, and hard cheese—took basil production into a commercial space.

Rice, Po Valley

The Po Valley's humid climate and marshes are the ideal environment for inhibiting weeds and cultivating rice. The region also supplies 50 percent of the European Union's rice.

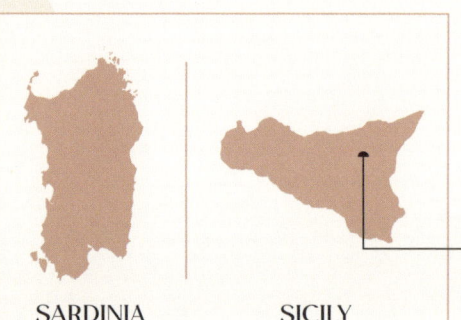

SARDINIA   SICILY

Citrus, Sicily

Citrus fruits, including lemons and oranges, abound in Sicily, where 64 percent of Italy's citrus is produced. They are the candied delight in the center of a *cannolo* and the sweet in a salad with fennel and olives.

Radicchio, Treviso
Adorned with white-and-purple striped wisps, radicchio is bitter in salads and a great addition to risotto. Produced in the Veneto city of Treviso, the plant cowers at the first frost and is harvested in midwinter.

Black truffles, Umbria
Sniffed out in oak and hazel forests by curly-haired Lagotto Romagnolo dogs, these "black diamonds" sell for €1,000 per kilogram, at times more. They're at their peak in fall, and are often shaved over poached eggs or fresh *strangozzi* pasta.

Olive oil, Puglia
More olive oil—essential in so many dishes—is produced in Puglia than in any other Italian region. Olives are picked in fall and pressed to a golden hue, the subtle color varying depending on the variety.

Tropea onions, Calabria
Woven into braids during the summer, the red Tropea onion (also known as Torpedo for its shape) is grown on Calabria's west coast. It's eaten raw, fried, on pasta, in a savory pie, or as a marmalade.

San Marzano tomatoes, Campania
Neapolitan pizza sauce is made from San Marzano tomatoes, which are sweetened by the mineral-rich volcanic soil found in the town of San Marzano sul Sarno. These fruits are believed to have arrived in Campania in the 18th century as a gift from the Kingdom of Peru.

ITALIAN GARDENS

Mastering nature with an Italian flair

As much a part of the landscape as the Alps or the Amalfi coastline, Italy's gardens are living celebrations of the natural world. Whether a manicured Renaissance estate or a small plot left to grow wild and wonderful, these gardens are every bit as beautiful as the paintings in the Uffizi. Their fascinating history speaks of Italy's changing relationship with the botanical world.

The roots of the garden

Picture the scene: a fragrant herb garden is framed by marble columns and rows of fruit trees, each providing shade from the Mediterranean sun. Sit on a stone bench, hear the lull of an ornate fountain, and see swooning swifts overhead. Sounds peaceful, doesn't it? The Romans certainly thought so. Gardens were ubiquitous in the Roman world. If part of a humble home, they were practical, used to cultivate produce, and provide the household with a source of income. If part of a grand estate, they were an earthly paradise, an extension of the home, and a way to show off wealth. The aristocrats and emperors who commissioned these grand estate gardens were influenced by Greek and Egyptian design, and their gardens followed Classical ideals of beauty and order, often organized around fountains and filled with statues, aviaries, and tree-lined walkways.

With the fall of the Roman Empire and subsequent fall in wealth (not to mention the increase in famine), gardens became primarily practical in the Middle Ages. The rise of

"If you have a library with a garden, you have everything you need."

Marcus Tulius Cicero

Back in 46 BCE, Marcus Tulius Cicero included this sentence in his *To Varro, in Ad Familiares IX*. It's a welcome reminder that for millennia, reading a good book in a quiet garden has been considered one of life's simplest pleasures.

monasticism led to the creation of monastic gardens and cloisters, which were often enclosed by high walls; they became places of peace once more but were also a means of survival, devoted to the growing of fruits and vegetables.

Political theater and pleasure

But it didn't take long for the garden to return to its elevated status. The Renaissance brought with it a huge rise in wealth, and nobility from warring city-states commissioned summer palaces with expansive

NOTABLE ITALIAN GARDENS

1538
Cosimo I de' Medici commissions a garden for his Florence residence, the Villa di Castello.

1549
Work starts on the Boboli Gardens, Florence's best example of stylized gardening.

1560
Architect Pirro Ligorio starts work on Villa d'Este, steeply terraced gardens and fountains in Tivoli, near Rome.

1671
A formal Baroque garden is created on Isola Bella, Lake Maggiore.

1753
Caserta Palace garden in Naples combines ornamental waterworks and statuary.

gardens. Offering more time for leisure and study, the Renaissance set off a renewed interest in the ornamental gardens of the ancient world. Gardens became grander, inspired by order and filled with features that showed off the wealth of their owners and evoked awe in visitors. Perhaps the greatest example of this opulence is the Villa d'Este in Tivoli, which would serve as the model for European gardens to come. Influenced by Rome, the ambitious garden was built to rival Hadrian's Villa by sourcing marble and statues from its ruins. Designed on a steep 11 acres (4.5 ha), its system of pools, 51 fountains, and multiple cascades was fed by the Aniene River using canals and underground pipes. The role of fountains as a symbol of power and status wasn't new, but Villa d'Este took it to new heights, with water powering musical instruments and roaring over cascades.

If impressing visitors was the goal, the Medicis perfected this during their several-hundred-year rule. Of the 16 estates with gardens that they amassed in Tuscany, Florence's Boboli Gardens are arguably the finest, a statement of grandeur that acts as a checklist of Italian Renaissance garden features: crisp geometric lines, carefully clipped hedges, and exuberant grottoes. At both Boboli and Villa d'Este, dukes and duchesses frolicked

Previous page Renaissance landscaping at the Boboli Gardens, Florence
Clockwise from top left Fountain of the Tripod spewing water at Villa d'Este, Tivoli; views at Villa d'Este; the gardens of Ninfa encroaching on medieval ruins

LAND AND WATER

It was in Italy that terrestrial plants were first grown underwater. In Liguria, Nemo's Garden uses desalinated seawater to nourish air-filled hydroponic biospheres and grow the likes of basil.

in grottoes, climbed terraced stairs, ducked in pergolas, and followed parterres and labyrinths to lavish fountains, as visitors still can today.

Contemporary gardens

Though these gardens remain, today Italy is dotted with wild and wonderful displays that represent the 20th-century departure from the perfect hedge. Nature is seemingly left to do its thing at Giardini di Ninfa, where plantings cascade over the crumbling ruins of the medieval village of Ninfa. Here, a luxurious combination of flowering trees, shrubs, and perennials might look unplanned and natural, but they were actually ingeniously planted to create a dreamy English landscape-style garden.

Whether stylized or wild, in vogue or redefining fashion, gardens are yet another way that Italians strive to make their world utterly beautiful.

1921 An English-style oasis garden takes over the abandoned medieval village of Ninfa.

1930 An American countess creates Rome's Rose Garden, home to more than a thousand species of the flower.

1958 Tropical and Mediterranean plants fill Ischia's La Mortella, a private garden at the time.

1988 Lombardy's Giardino Botanico Fondazione André Heller brings art installations and plants together.

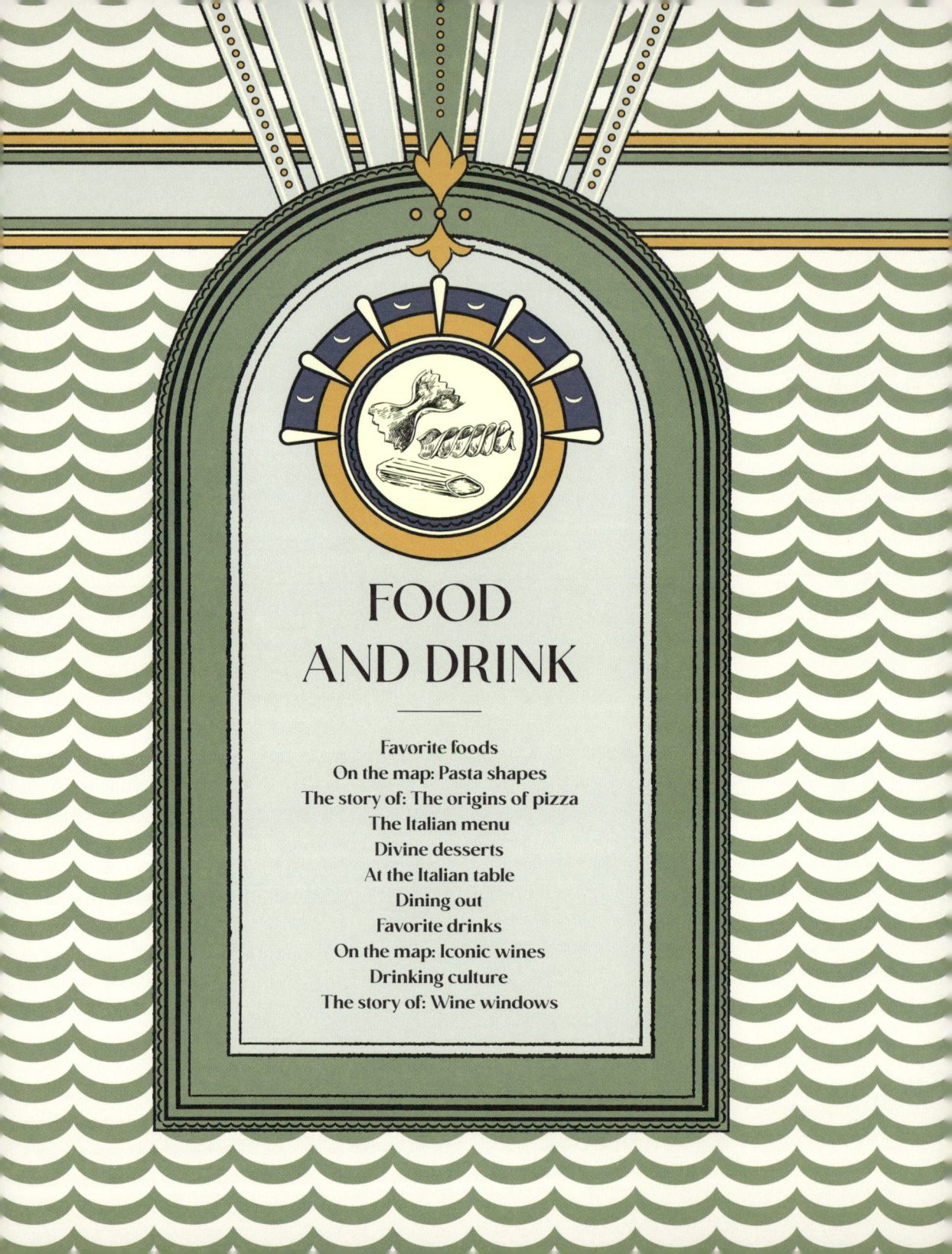

FOOD
AND DRINK

~~~~~~~~~

Italian food needs no introduction. Pizza, pasta, gelato—these are foods so delicious that they've become some of the world's most loved. After all, they're the very definition of comfort and familiarity, whether you're cooking up a hearty pasta dish or tucking in to an epic pizza on the weekend. And there's no end to the tasty foods Italians have perfected: salty cured meats, creamy cheeses, warming risottos, and fresh seafood, all lovingly prepared and inspired by family recipes. Then there are the drinks we know and love. Always order a negroni on a night out? Thank Florence. Love to sip a Chianti red with dinner? That's down to Florence's eponymous neighbor. And the refreshing spritz you order as soon as summer hits? Venice is behind that. Oh, and if a Moka pot sits on your kitchen shelves, that's Italy too—its coffee scene is second to none. When all is said and done, it's little wonder Italy's food and drinks are on menus far and wide.

~~~~~~~~~

FAVORITE FOODS

Icons of Italian cuisine

Pizza, pasta, risotto, gelato—these dishes are such familiar favorites that we rarely pause to reflect on how they came to be. Wildly varied, beautifully simple, and honed over thousands of years, Italy's menu is the result of fresh, local ingredients fine-tuned to perfection. There are few better cures for a somber mood than a dish from Italy's extensive menu—it's no wonder these foods are loved the world over.

Perfect pasta

Perhaps Italy's most celebrated export, pasta is the humble hero of the Italian pantry. It might be ubiquitous across the country, but pasta has countless origin stories. Some believe that the explorer Marco Polo brought pasta back to Italy from his travels in China, but records suggest that a steaming bowl of the stuff was enjoyed here long before Polo's adventures; there is firm evidence of the Etruscans cooking and eating pasta in Italy as early 400 BCE.

In the Middle Ages, simple pasta was one of those rare foods that was loved by rich and poor alike, with recipes varying depending on one's social standing. And during the decadent days of the European Grand Tour in the 18th century, young English aristocrats returned with one thing on their mind (and, often, dried in their suitcase): pasta. So began a global love affair that shows no sign of waning.

You could travel across the whole of Italy and learn a potted history of its regions through its pasta dishes. *Spaghetti alle vongole*, spaghetti with clams, can be traced back to the coastal regions of Naples, where clams have been harvested for over 9,000 years. Carbonara—spaghetti tossed with a sauce of raw beaten eggs, topped with crispy cured *guanciale* meat—is associated with the Lazio region, but some connect it to *pasta cacio e uova*, a Neapolitan dish of pasta tossed with melted lard, beaten raw eggs, and cheese. Sicily's *pasta alla norma*, a small taste of southern summer on a plate, combines penne *rigate*, eggplant, and tomato, with a healthy smattering of *ricotta salata* and basil. Today, there are more than 350 defined shapes of pasta (*p82*), and surely too many recipes to count.

Rice dishes

Though every region has its signature pasta (and sauces), in the north of Italy rice-based risotto is as prevalent as pasta, and even takes its place as a first course. Rice was introduced to Italy's northern regions from Asia in

~

Clockwise from left
Getting hands-on in
the kitchen; making
fresh *orecchiette*,
traditional pasta;
straining home-
made gnocchi

~~~~~~~~~~~~~~~~~~~~~~~~~~

THE BEST BOLOGNESE

Ragù alla Bolognese, or Bolognese
sauce, is a meat-based sauce
originating in the city of Bologna. The
origins of Bolognese sauce are believed
to date back to the late 18th century,
with the first recorded reference to a
meat sauce served with pasta. The
sauce we know and love today is
made with ground meat, onions,
and fresh tomatoes.

~~~~~~~~~~~~~~~~~~~~~~~~~~

the Middle Ages, but it was pioneering home cooks from Lombardy, Piedmont, and Veneto who invented the classic risotto we know and love today. The genius is in its creamy texture, created by slowly simmering the rice in stock. There are countless varieties of risotto, but the classic has to be *risotto alla Milanese.* Here, the grains are simmered with onions, wine, and saffron, which gives them a light yellow hue, before the dish is topped with butter and cheese. Other risotto varieties include mushroom, seafood or, as the temperatures fall around fall, pumpkin.

Never eager to fit in the with the rest of the country, southern Italians took the humble risotto and put their own spin on it. A staple of Sicilian cuisine, arancini involves rolling risotto into a ball, stuffing it with meat or cheese, covering it in bread crumbs and deep frying it into a small ball of divine goodness. It's so tasty, just one ball is never quite enough.

Anyone for pizza?

Risotto and pasta are seared in the global consciousness as quintessential Italian dishes, but ask someone to name their favorite Italian food and they'll inevitably say one thing: pizza. With around half a dozen types in Italy, from thin crust to thick *pizza al taglio* (served by the slice), pizza is something of an umbrella term for an array of doughy delights with any number of toppings.

But which is best? For many Italians, the only true pizza is a Neapolitan margherita. For that mouthwatering creation, a *pizzaiolo* artfully tosses a dough disc in the air to create the base, tops it with sauce made from San Marzano tomatoes—grown in the rich soil of Mount Vesuvius—and

mozzarella cheese, fires it for 90 seconds in a wood-burning oven, and garnishes it with basil. The margherita is delivered hot and uncut with a fluffy yet crunchy crust and thin center. And it's simply too good to share.

As with so many Italian dishes, the pizza (*p84*) is a simple celebration of the very best produce. The building blocks of the dish—tomatoes, olive oil, mozzarella, and garlic—are the cornerstones of so many Italian wonders, their delicate flavors capturing the essence of Italy.

Ciabatta and focaccia

Pizza might be Italy's doughy treat of choice, but the country's bakeries turn out a host of great breads, giving the French *boulangeries* a run for their

~~~

Above left One of Florence's popular sandwich shops
Above right A classic margherita
Right Prepping Sicilian street food at Santa Rosalia festival

money. There's a good reason Italians describe people of strong character as being like a piece of bread (*"Essere un pezzo di pane"*)—bread is a humble, reliable, and much-loved fixture of the table.

A favorite has to be focaccia, an ancient bread that is thought to have originated with the Etruscans. Its name is derived from the Latin *panis focacius*, meaning "hearth bread," as it was once cooked over hot coals. Made from a simple dough and topped with an array of treats—rosemary, sage, garlic, cheese, or a sweet version with honey, raisins, sugar, and lemon peel—it has a fluffy texture, ideal for soaking up flavors.

While the long history of focaccia stretches back to ancient times, Italy's

other favorite bread, ciabatta, has been around for only a few decades. The ciabatta was invented by a baker in Rome in 1982 as a proud Italian alternative to the French baguette (its name means "slipper" in Italian due to its long shape). Ciabatta is baked with a high level of hydration, making the holes within the dough much bigger than the French equivalent. It's used in a variety of ways, but perhaps the most popular use is in the panini, a grilled sandwich that gained huge popularity after it became a fixture of Italian American delis.

The land and the seasons

Aside from the staples of pizza, rice, and pasta, Italy's menu is a varied celebration of seasonal vegetables and local meats. And when it comes to sourcing the best of the land's bounty, it pays to work with the seasons. Summer is the time of the raw tomato, when Italian tables are loaded with fresh and colorful *caprese* salads—mozzarella, ripe tomatoes, basil, olive oil—and delicious *panzanella*, a Tuscan salad made with stale bread, tomatoes, onions, cucumbers, and basil. These lighter offerings might accompany an epic meat centerpiece: in Tuscany, *bistecca alla Fiorentina* is a local favorite. What makes this T-bone steak different, aside from the fact that it's sourced from local Chianina cattle, is that it's cooked on a wood-fired grill, before being served rare in a portion designed for sharing—the serving typically weighs in at a belt-busting 2.2 lb (1 kg).

As the Italian sun begins to fade, home cooks preserve the summer's bounty, filling their pantry with jarred tomatoes, peppers, and anchovies. Winter also sees a host of comforting dishes. Polenta is a warming winter

staple made from ground cornmeal, typically boiled in water or milk before roasting as an accompaniment to meat or fish. This is also the time of hearty soups, like the Tuscan favorite *ribbolita*. A fine example of *cucina povera* (recipes that originated from Italy's rural peasant populations), the soup is packed with winter vegetables and thickened with day-old bread. A dish to banish those winter blues, if ever there was one.

The sea's bounty

Farming and a focus on seasonal produce are essential to Italian cooking, but with its vast stretches of coast, fishing is just as prevalent. Every region has its specialties: eels and clams are favored along the Adriatic coast, while central Italian seafood revolves around anchovies, sardines, and tuna. For a favorite restaurant starter, mixed seafood is battered and fried: simple, decadent, divine, like the best of Italy's menu.

Above Shelves stocked with Italian pantry staples, like jars of preserved fish and vegetables

EDOARDO CELADON

— ◦◦◦ —

On the beauty of the Italian food system

Former chef and entrepreneur Edoardo Celadon founded Most of Italy to preserve and celebrate his country's ethical approach to food. We all know and love Italy for the simplicity of its dishes, but for Celadon, appreciating the country's cuisine means looking well beyond the plate. In fact, it means leaving the kitchen entirely and venturing back to the fields, forests, and oceans where the country's staple ingredients are sourced. By arranging unique gastronomic experiences, Most of Italy raises awareness of the thousands of dedicated farmers, fishers, and growers who stock Italy's kitchens and pantries.

"I used to be a self-trained cook," Celadon says. "I realized food in most restaurants wasn't the food I wanted people to eat. So I stepped out of the kitchen and started researching Italian farmers—I traveled all across the country. I'm interested in the journey from field to seed to harvest to plate, and I want people to join me in these journeys." In Celadon's view, the beauty of Italian cuisine begins well before the *soffrito* or the careful seasoning of the sauce. "Italy is famous for the way we *cook*, but we should also be famous for the way we *produce*. We have the

cleanest agriculture on earth. If there is one thing that Italy has left to teach the world, it's how to be a farmer, and how to preserve our landscapes."

Those Italian chefs arguing heatedly over the correct way to cook a carbonara might be surprised to hear this, but Celadon believes we pay too much attention to specifics, without considering the food system as a whole. "We need to forget about closely guarding recipes; we need to focus on protecting ingredients."

Through his company, he has taken visitors on tours to the heart of the Italian food system, arranging trips with truffle hunters, dinners on small Tuscan farms and boat rides with sustainable fishers, all with the aim of enhancing the voices of those who feed the country. He recognizes that many Italians are fiercely protective of their culinary heritage, but knows that more needs to be done if these traditions are to thrive in the modern age. This is not about ripping up the recipe book or reducing the talents of the country's chefs but about broadening the picture to take in the larger systems that put food on the table. By taking these journeys, he suggests, that first bite of spaghetti will taste all the richer.

PASTA SHAPES

If all of life is "a combination of magic and pasta," as Italian film director Federico Fellini once whimsically put it, then the *maestro*'s home country sure has a competitive edge. Fresh or dry, tubular or ribbony, filled or flat, pasta remains Italy's favorite food, but it's never *just* a base layer for spotlight-stealing sauce. All shapes are very much *not* created equal, and most are highly localized; pairing rules can border on the dogmatic, though reigning expert Oretta Zanini de Vita, author of *Encyclopedia of Pasta*, has controversially said that "any sauce goes decently well with any shape." Here are just a few standouts.

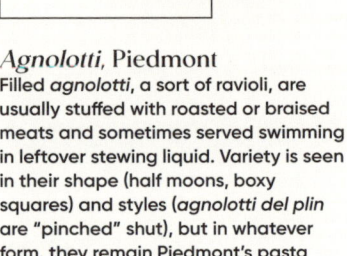

Casarecce, Sicily
A durum wheat pasta that resembles a convoluted papyrus scroll, *casarecce* are widely believed to have originated in Arab nations. Their Italian homeland, Sicily, has always been a crossroads of civilizations. And just as Sicily pulls from a mix of cultures, ultra-versatile *casarecce* work with many sauces.

Agnolotti, Piedmont
Filled *agnolotti*, a sort of ravioli, are usually stuffed with roasted or braised meats and sometimes served swimming in leftover stewing liquid. Variety is seen in their shape (half moons, boxy squares) and styles (*agnolotti del plin* are "pinched" shut), but in whatever form, they remain Piedmont's pasta *de rigueur*.

Pappardelle, Tuscany
Though associated with Tuscany, these days *pappardelle*'s reach is as wide as their ribbon. The root word is *pappare*—to nosh or gobble up—and this is the inevitable outcome when served with wild boar (*cinghiale*).

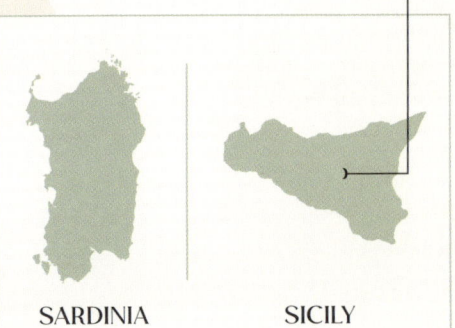

SARDINIA   SICILY

Bigoli, Veneto

Rice and polenta might be the main grains in Veneto, but the region is hardly a pasta wasteland. Thick, spaghetti-like *bigoli* are the area's signature style and are most often served *in salsa* (an umami blitz of anchovy and onion that's far more satiating than it is photogenic).

Tortellini, Emilia-Romagna

Bologna proudly wears its title of *tortellini* capital, particularly at Christmas, when *tortellini* in broth are a table mainstay. This meat- or vegetable-stuffed egg pasta, in its finest, freshest form, is often tinier than non-Italians imagine it to be, though the diminutive "-ini" is the first clue that they should look more dainty than dumplingy.

Spaghetti chitarra, Abruzzo

What's a guitar *(chitarra)* got to do with this square-edged spaghetti from central Italy? The reference doesn't come from the stringy form of the egg pasta itself, but from the specialized wire-and-wood tool used to craft it—a staple in the kitchens of all culinary rock stars between Teramo and Chieti.

Orecchiette, Puglia

Orecchiette directly translates to "little ears," owing to this oddly kitschy pasta's distinct shape. A coarse, crinkled surface, compressed center and upturned edges make them the perfect mini-spoons for savory *cime di rapa* (the leafy green vegetable, rapini); in Puglia, the two go together like bread and butter.

Bucatini, Lazio

With a name that alludes to the holes at the end of these long, narrow tubes, *bucatini* could seem gimmicky if they weren't so good. They crop up all over Lazio, but have special ties to the tiny, quasi-lost town of Amatrice, which lends its name to one of the pasta's best pairing sauces—peppery *amatriciana*, made with *guanciale*, tomato, *pecorino romano*, olive oil, and white wine.

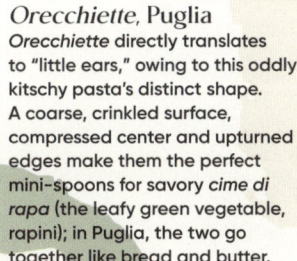

THE ORIGINS OF PIZZA

Pizza is one of Italy's most celebrated exports, yet its ancient origins are hazy. A fresco unearthed at Pompeii is thought to depict a 2,000-year-old pizza prototype, though even earlier pizzalike dishes were actually a Greek invention, with the ancient Greeks' "pissa" breads—a cross between today's pita breads and pizza—found across the Mediterranean.

They may have been inspired by Greece, but Italians sure perfected the pizza we know and love today. Naples produced the first modern pizza in the early 18th century by baking bread smeared in pork fat and cheese. In 1760, Neapolitans started adding tomatoes, which had recently arrived from the Americas. The fruit was first viewed with suspicion by haughty Europeans more accustomed to a meat-heavy diet, but the frugal Neapolitans were known as *"mangiafoglia"* (leaf-eaters) because of their poverty-driven reliance on vegetables, and they were quick to embrace the juicy red tomato. Early pizza fans also added other humble toppings like garlic, olive oil, and salt.

Word swiftly spread through Italy and beyond. Just like today, trying Neapolitan pizza became an essential activity for Grand Tour travelers. Then came the grandest tourist of all: in 1899, Italy's Queen Margherita visited Naples and asked to try pizza. Her topping of tomato, mozzarella, and basil—supposedly to match the colors of the Italian flag—became the definitive margherita pizza. The rest, of course, is history.

> "They may have been inspired by Greece, but Italians sure perfected the pizza we know and love today."

Left A hot pizza, fresh out of the oven

THE ITALIAN MENU

Good food comes to those who wait

Italian dining novices, a word of warning: mealtimes are a marathon, not a sprint. Here, the menu is split into a unique running order: *aperitivi, antipasti, primi, secondi*—and that's before you get to the sweet stuff. So if your host serves or orders you a bowl of pasta, take it slow and don't ask for seconds. Enjoying food slowly and in the right order is a key part of the dining experience, and each course is intended to complement those that came before and follow after. To make the most of the Italian menu, a small amount of decoding—and a good deal of pacing—is key.

Aperitivo and antipasti

Ever wondered why many Italians eat so late? It's because the *aperitivo*—the predinner drink that sets the meal in motion—is worth lingering over. The tradition dates back to the wise medics of ancient Greece, who recommended bitter wines to awaken the appetite. And Italians still meet long before dinner (either at the restaurant itself or at a bar nearby) for a beer, wine, spirit, or liqueur. Putting the world to rights over a small drink and a plate of crackers and olives or meats, cheeses, and breads is the perfect prelude to the meal itself. Italians know to go easy on this first leg—there are many further treats in store.

The predinner drink is followed by the *antipasti*, a heavier starter than the nibbles that came before. Ancient Romans coined the term *antipasto* (literally "before the meal") and were known to enjoy this course as part of their own elaborate banquets. The *antipasti* may consist of a charcuterie platter loaded with salame, mortadella,

L'appetito vien mangiando

Appetite comes while you are eating

The extensive and lengthy Italian menu is guided by the belief that appetite should be satiated slowly, with every dish building to a grand finale. Some Italians might (semi-jokingly) say their hunger builds over the first few courses, as they look ahead to the main event.

> "Preparing and roasting meat for the secondi course varies by region."

or prosciutto and accompanied with cheeses. Other options might include cold, cured fish like tuna or salmon. The small plates are perfectly designed to whet your appetite for the hot dishes to come.

Primi

This course is the first time you'll find hot food served, and it typically celebrates carbohydrates in all their wonder: think pasta or rice. Pasta has always been a light starter or an accompaniment on the table, but during the 19th century, Italy flirted with having it as a main course—which is how many people around the world enjoy it today.

The pasta possibilities are, of course, endless. And depending where you are, it can be a great way to sample a local specialty: in Tuscany, perhaps pappardelle with ragù (wild boar); in Liguria, *trofie* with *pesto alla Genovese*; in Emilia-Romagna, especially in the fall, sage and butter-topped *tortelli di zucca* (filled with pumpkin). Then there's gnocchi—soft, fat, and chewy dumplings served with pesto or a tomato-based sauce, a great option all over the country. Whatever you choose, you can rarely go wrong here.

Not that you have to order pasta. In the north, and especially in Lombardy and the Po Valley where rice is rich, a fresh risotto is a common *primo*.

Secondi

Carnivores rejoice: the *secondi* is the first meat-forward, protein-heavy course of the evening, when glorious hunks of local beef, pork, lamb, or other meats or fish are served steaming hot and ready for slicing.

Preparing and roasting meat for the *secondi* course varies significantly by region. Take roast beef, for example, which differs in both name and method across Italy: in Naples, it's called *biffo*, while in Parma you might hear the more familiar sirloin. Further confusion arises when considering the cuts of meat, as there is no general classification across Italy; knowing your rump from your topside in one region may not prepare you for a host of different names used elsewhere.

While the previous courses have changed subtly over Italy's long history, with *primi* and *antipasti* offerings becoming more varied, the *secondi* tethers Italians to their

~~

Previous page
Alfresco dining
in Rome
Above Plating
up a meaty *secondi*
Right A selection
of cheeses and fruit

ancient past. Meat has long been served as the grand finale of the savory courses, due largely to the belief that the heaviest elements should be enjoyed last.

All is not lost for vegetarians and vegans, by the way. Italian chefs can turn even the humblest vegetables into main offerings worthy of the *secondi* course. Few can say where eggplant *parmigiana* comes from (with many regions claiming it as their own), but most are agreed that this layered dish of tomato, eggplant, and mozzarella is a worthy rival to any roast meat.

Contorni and insalata

The *secondi* course, in whatever form, needs something to accompany it, and that's where the *contorni* come in. These side dishes are light, fresh, raw, and vegetarian, to offset the heaviness of the meat and cleanse the palate. Legumes like lentils, fava beans, peas, and chickpeas are often featured on the *contorni* page of the menu. *Secondi* dishes might also be served alongside a small and simple side salad (*insalata*)—a handful of fresh leaves, ripe tomatoes, a pinch of salt, and drizzle of olive oil—though salads can also be enjoyed as a dish in themselves, particularly in summer.

Formaggi and frutta

We're nearing the end of the meal, and it's customary to take a welcome pause after the *secondi*, to prolong the dinner experience. Not everyone takes a break, though; at larger gatherings and celebrations, a board of cheese and fruit often comes out, providing a great opportunity to revel in the country's 2,500 types of cheese (that's more than France). Typically, hard, semihard, and soft varieties all are featured, with a roll call of some of the world's favorite cheeses—gorgonzola, taleggio, burrata, mozzarella, mascarpone, parmigiano reggiano—all served alongside fresh, local fruit.

Did you think it was all over? There's still one more course to go, and the best is saved for last: bring on the *dolce*. And Italy's incredible dessert menu is a story in its own right.

DIVINE DESSERTS

The sweeter side of life

Italy's main courses might be globally renowned, but the fun certainly doesn't stop with the last forkful of *spaghetti pomodoro*. The country is also home to some of the world's favorite sweet treats—gelato, *tiramisù*, panettone, and ricotta-filled cannoli, to name just a few. Stumbling upon seasonal and regional desserts—sometimes specific to a town or saint's day—is a particular delight. Made with as much love and pride as the rest of the meal, Italian dessert recipes are usually simple at the core and yet deliciously indulgent.

Frozen joys

Of all the desserts across Italy, gelato is the perennial favorite. Silkier than regular ice cream, churned at a slightly warmer temperature, and made without egg, it has a smooth texture that allows the flavors to shine through. Italians are sticklers for what makes a proper gelato: fresh fruit, some good-quality dairy, and traditional techniques (steer well clear of the touristy gelato shops with technicolor mounds of ice cream piled high). Gelato tends to be something that's eaten out and about as a treat, rather than made at home, with classic flavors including *stracciatella*—a vanilla or plain milk flavor with crunchy chocolate flakes and pistachio, sometimes sprinkled with whole chunks of nuts.

Another frozen wonder is *sorbetto*, or sorbet, which is made without dairy and ideally with fresh fruit. Artisanal *gelaterias* will have seasonal flavors like blackberry, apricot, and peach on the menu, as well as more unusual creations like basil or mulberry. *Affogato* is another post-dinner delight, a scoop of gelato atop an espresso providing a great hot-and-cold combination.

Divine and decadent

Sticking on the theme of coffee-related treats, there's not much that trumps a classic *tiramisù*. This crowd-pleasing dessert is made with layers of lady-finger sponge biscuits—Savoiardi or Pavesini, depending on who you ask—dipped into a shot of fresh espresso, a lightly whipped *zabaglione* and mascarpone, and a thick coating of cocoa powder. Most say the dessert was first made in the 1960s in Veneto, though various stories about its creation abound, including one that claims it was developed as a popular aphrodisiac. Fittingly, then, the name loosely translates as "pick me up,"

perhaps because of its supposed "restorative" properties.

For those who don't like coffee, there's the triflelike cousin, *zuppa inglese*, made with blood-red *alchermes* liqueur and custard. In some places, you'll even find a fruity variation of *tiramisù* made with persimmon and sweet wine.

Festive flavors

Not far away from the hometown of *tiramisù*, another iconic Italian dessert was born several centuries earlier: panettone. The Italian alternative to Christmas cake is a light-as-can-be enriched dough filled with currants, candied peel, and dried fruit. At Easter, a similar version of panettone comes out in the form of *colomba*, shaped like a dove and sprinkled with almonds.

And with that welcome burst of sweetness, the meal concludes—though these *dolci* can be enjoyed whenever, such is the Italian way.

Above left *Tiramisù* dusted with cocoa powder
Above right Enjoying some gelato

THE STORY OF
Gelato

Gelato is everywhere in Italy, but Florentines claim that the dessert was born in their city. As the story goes, architect Bernardo Buontalenti was tasked with organizing a grand banquet for the Medici court in 1559 and invented a new dessert for the occasion: a chilled treat flavored with citrus. Gelato quickly spread across the city and beyond, and the rest is delicious history.

AT THE ITALIAN TABLE

The rules and traditions of meal times

Italian dishes might be beautiful in and of themselves, but they are best enjoyed as part of the wider social ritual of the Italian table. Defined by long-acknowledged conventions, eating together is a serious business in Italy. This is not to say that a meal is ever a tediously formal affair, as anyone who has spent a languorous evening around an Italian table can attest. Rather, these time-honored traditions serve to enhance the simple joys of eating well.

Ancient rituals

Italians have been perfecting their table manners for over 2,000 years, with ancient Romans particularly fond of hosting elaborate banquets. The consumption of food and drink was a vital social ritual, with banquets known as *convivium* (Latin for "living together"). The Romans had a glossary for different meals, each bound by their own small codes: the *epulum* (public feast), the *cena* (the midafternoon dinner), and the *comissatio* (the drinking party).

This long lineage of dining customs is one reason why Italy's table rituals may seem confusing to an outsider, bound up as they are with centuries of social history.

Beyond etiquette

Once food is served, the loosely choreographed theater of the Italian meal begins. It's standard practice to wait for everyone to be served before starting to eat, to never turn the bread upside down or spill salt or oil, to show a hearty appetite and finish your plate, to drink wine but not get drunk, to never ask for

---
~~~
---

## *A tavola non si invecchia*

### One doesn't age at the table

Pointing to the magic of mealtimes in Italy, this oft-repeated phrase captures how the moments spent sharing meals with loved ones are too happy to wear us down; instead, the worries of life fade away with good food and good company.

---
~~~

Right Tucking in
at the table

Parmesan cheese on seafood dishes, to compliment the cook repeatedly and effusively.

If there's ever a time when these table rules are played out most keenly, it's Sunday lunch. The *pranzo della domenica* is a multihour, multigenerational affair that brings together families (and today, often friends). The meal is still bound by the unspoken rule that one should eat enough at this hallowed lunch to remain full for the rest of the week. This was once an insurance policy in the event that food became scarce, but it lives on today as a welcome excuse for an indulgent feast.

A year at the table

Just as Italians mark the end of the week with Sunday dinner, so do they mark the passing of the year with a calendar of sacred meals. From the lavish spreads of Christmas Eve to the sociable table settings on Ferragosto (*p146*), celebrations and their dishes are inseparable. For Easter Sunday, lamb symbolizes renewal, while the Feast of the Seven Fishes on Christmas Eve in Rome and much of the south uses an age-old practice of eating seafood on holidays to mark the moment. On New Year's Eve, lentils are served at midnight, a symbol of good fortune for the coming year, thought to have Roman origins. In a country that clings proudly to its past, holding onto traditional meals is a vital link to a slower and simpler era, and offers Italians a vital connection to their heritage.

Clockwise from below left Pumpkin ravioli; enjoying a meal; dining out in Pienza; a serving of pork sausage and lentils

DINING OUT

Seeing and being seen at the Italian restaurant

Given the choice, most Italians would struggle to pick between eating a hearty home-cooked feast or popping to their favorite restaurant. Both options are among life's simplest joys, but dining out is a cultural experience that goes far beyond the simple act of eating. Across Italy, friends gather at food markets, families congregate at the local trattoria, and lovers share spaghetti at candlelit restaurants. Food is one of the cornerstones of Italian society, and for every perfect dish, there's an ideal place to eat it.

From osteria to trattoria

In Italy, there are many different classifications of restaurants, each cultivating a different mood and serving a different kind of dish. That small, casual spot out of town with communal tables and a short, handwritten menu? That's an *osteria*, a cheap and unpretentious eatery where you can expect one or two humble dishes—spaghetti with local clams, say—served quickly.

Then there's the trattoria, a family-run restaurant, slightly larger and more formal than the *osteria*. When we picture dining in Italy, we're probably thinking of the trattoria: tables spread around a small terrace, wine bottles tucked into racks, and a perfectly curated menu of regional dishes. Many Italians will have been visiting their favorite local trattoria for decades, and they remain wonderfully social spaces.

Heading out for a birthday, anniversary, or festive celebration? That calls for the *ristorante*, a sophisticated eatery serving fine dishes and a choice selection of wines.

Pagare alla romana
To pay Roman style

Also known as *facciamo alla Romana*—meaning to split the bill equally—the phrase is said to hark back to the days when Roman eateries would divide the total due among large groups to simplify paying the bill.

Here, prices are higher, clothes are smarter, and great service is everything. This is also where many of the finer pieces of dining etiquette—known as *galateo*—come into play. Italians drink only water and wine with meals (no soft drinks or tea), for example, and it's customary to order the local specialty.

Perhaps the most popular of spots, however, is the neighborhood bar, the second most important place after home for many Italians. It's the beating heart of a *quartiere*, a place to keep abreast of local gossip, meet with old friends, and make new ones.

On the street

But dining out doesn't have to take place around a table. Street food in Italy dates back over 2,000 years, when ancient citizens would buy hot food from vendors at open-air markets. And just like buying popcorn at the movie theater today, a day out at the Colosseum wasn't complete without snacking on fried fish and salted peas. At ancient sites like Pompeii, preserved examples of these eateries can still be seen.

While street food today looks a little different to the salted peas of ancient Rome, it's still very much a feature of modern life. *Pizza al taglio* (pizza by the slice, or literally "cut pizza") originated in Rome in the 1950s: it's cut and sold by weight, with the customer dictating their preferred size. In Naples, where chefs are happy to fry just about anything, *pizza fritta* rules. Instead of being cooked in an oven, pizza is deep fried then topped with meat and cheese. This method was simply the most practical way to prepare a pizza without an oven—it's just perfect for serving from a food cart and devouring on the go.

Right An assortment of fried vegetables, meat, and seafood, a street food staple in Naples
Below Settling in for pizza and pasta at a café patio in Rome

FAVORITE DRINKS

Drinks to raise a glass (or two) to

The espresso you sip every morning, the Chianti you clink at dinner, and the negroni you order on a night out? That's Italy's influence. Italian life marks time in empty glasses, and fortunately, the locals have some of the greatest drinks to fill them with. Much like its food, these drinks reflect the country's rich landscape, culture, and traditions, with everything from wine to cocktails having been nurtured and perfected over centuries.

Fueled by coffee

Italy didn't invent coffee, but it may well be the bean's spiritual home. When Venetian botanist Prospero Alpini returned to Italy from Egypt carrying a coffee plant in 1580, he couldn't have imagined the revolution he would ignite. Soon *caffè*, from the Arabic *qahwah*, had established itself as the drink of choice for intellectuals and artisans, helped in large part by Pope Clement VIII, who gave the coffee bean his papal blessing in 1600. Coffeehouses sprang up rapidly from then, and in 1884, Angelo Moriondo patented the first coffee machine. When engineer Alfonso Bialetti emerged from the Alps clutching the world's first Moka pot in 1933, Italy's coffee revolution was complete.

As true now as it was then, days in Italy don't start until you've had an espresso (*un caffè*), traditionally served in a small cup with a saucer and a tiny spoon. Little surprise this is the default order: the espresso was invented here in 1903, when businessman Luigi Bezzera was frustrated with how long it took to make his cup of java and started experimenting with his machine's steam pressure. Other versions have developed since, from the shorter espresso *ristretto* to the milky macchiato, but the original is tough to beat. The second coffee of the day is

THE STORY OF
The Moka pot

The beautifully simple, octagonal-shaped Moka pot was invented in 1933 by designer Luigi di Ponti. The pot was then tweaked by a machinist from Piedmont, Alfonso Bialetti, who turned Ponti's design into the device we know and love today: a metal, pressure-driven stove-top coffee brewer. The device set in motion a home-brewing revolution, as coffee lovers could finally make a quality cup from their own kitchen.

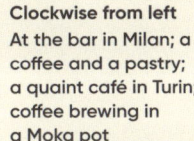

Clockwise from left
At the bar in Milan; a
coffee and a pastry;
a quaint café in Turin;
coffee brewing in
a Moka pot

~~

Left A *bicerin*
Below Examining
a red wine
Right Making a
classic spritz

the cappuccino, made with a dollop of milk glistened with foam. Fast on the heels of the espresso, it's usually enjoyed with a pastry before 11 a.m.

Much like food, regional varieties exist in the form of coffee, too. Turin's *bicerin* is a frilly confection of espresso, chocolate, milk, and cream, while the *moretta* is a rum-coffee bullet drink found almost exclusively in the northern part of Marche.

Italy's wine cellar

While coffee holds revered status in Italy, wine is the true lifeblood of the country. As important as water, wine isn't a luxury but a way of life; from rich, bold reds in Puglia and Piedmont to sparkling wines in Veneto and Lombardy, Italy has a wine for every taste. The peninsula's first wine was produced around the 7th century BCE, when the Etruscans tinkered in the hills of central Italy using methods learned from the Greeks. The Romans gradually took over, turning wine production into an industry that spread across the empire. In ancient Rome, *vino* was viewed as a gift from Bacchus, the god of wine, who was honored and worshipped with wild parties fueled by barrels of the good stuff. The empire's collapse in 476 CE brought with it a halt in wine production until the Renaissance; just as important as the revival of art and science in this period was that of wine, an often undervalued contribution of Europe's rebirth.

Italian wine is certainly worth worshipping a higher power for, but what, exactly, makes the country's *vino* so special? That'd be Italy itself, a subcontinent of landscapes each with their own unique terroir and grape varieties. The result of a warm climate and sunshine is an outstanding level of

glass of Chianti. It's thought that the Phoenicians first traded and consumed beer in Sicily in the 7th century BCE, with the ancient Romans going one step further to produce the drink themselves, albeit in small amounts. From the onset of the Renaissance, beer was mostly imported; the country's agricultural soil meant that grapes for wine-making grew far easier than hops and grains needed for beer brewing.

But this didn't deter one of Italy's most iconic producers, Birra Moretti. In the northern town of Udine in 1859, entrepreneur Ligui Moretti figured he'd make more money producing beer locally than importing it from breweries within the Austro-Hungarian empire. He opened his own brewery, sold the first bottle of Moretti beer to the region in 1860, and was distributing across the entire country by the 1990s. Though it's since encountered fierce competitors, it's still a house-hold name around the world today.

In the spirit

When something a little stronger is required, Italian spirits are a winner. Many spirits were first produced in the Middle Ages, when monks created medicinal concoctions and herbal liqueurs that developed into the spirits that line bars today. Grappa, mostly served in the northeast, is one of the earliest spirits produced in Italy—and one so good it's inspired villages in the Veneto to add "del Grappa" to their name, notably Bassano del Grappa. Conjured out of the leftover grape skins, pulp, and seeds from wine-making, it developed a side hustle as a coffee "corrector," added to espressos to give them a kick.

diversity: the complex orange wines of Gorizia, the golden Ambrosia of the Valdobbiadene, the fruity reds of Chianti, and the sweet wine of Marsala, to name just a few. The golden rule of creating such great wine is an excellent grape harvest, with grapes across the country being harvested in the winter before they're crushed, fermented, and aged.

With such a vast assortment of wines to choose from, deciding which bottle to open often depends on the dish you're drinking it with. A light, fragrant Vernaccia white pairs perfectly with a seafood dish, for example, while a sweet Sangiovese is ideal for rich pasta dishes.

Brewing beer

Italian wine might steal the limelight, but beer isn't an afterthought here—it's as refreshing on a sunny day as any

NOTABLE MOMENTS IN WINE HISTORY

700s BCE
The Greeks introduce viticulture to Sicily.

100s CE
The Roman wine trade thrives, with vineyards spreading across the empire.

500s
After the Romans, winemaking is managed by monks.

1420s
Renaissance winemaking introduces new Tuscan classics.

1800s
Phylloxera epidemic devastates Italy's vineyards.

1960s
New laws regulate winemaking, increasing the quality of *vino*.

Another renowned liqueur is limoncello, a tangy drink made from lemons, typically served chilled as a digestivo after a meal. Native to the south, limoncello is mostly made along the Amalfi Coast and has a slightly bitter, sweet, and zesty taste.

Shaking it up

While many Italian spirits are best enjoyed neat to fully appreciate their flavor, they're also the base for some of the world's most loved cocktails. One of the most popular is the spritz, the orange glow of which must have drawn Venetians like moths to a flame when it first debuted in the 1920s. It's really just Prosecco, soda water, and bitters, a recipe partially influenced by the old Austrian habit of spraying (*spritzen* in German) fizzy water into wine to dilute it. From these rather pithy origins, the spritz transformed into the drink we know and love today. Milan's contribution to the spritz comes in the form of Campari, first concocted in 1860. Its bold flavor derives from a blend of herbs, spices, and fruits, resulting in a bittersweet taste with a hint of citrus. The exact ingredients remain a closely guarded secret, and it has a long-running rivalry with Padua's Aperol as the bitters of choice for the spritz.

The Venetian cocktail renaissance also gave us the Bellini, invented by chef Giuseppe Cipriani and named after the 15th-century painter Giovanni Bellini. A whimsy of Prosecco and peach purée, it's an aesthetically pleasing cocktails, associated with the elegance of the Venetian lifestyle. Really, that level of sophistication extends to all drinks in Italy, offering up the opportunity to sip something great and indulge in *dolce far niente,* the art of doing nothing.

Above Spirits lining the shelves of a stylish bar in Palermo
Left Limoncello, made in the south

LINDSAY GABBARD

— ∿ —

On fine Italian wine and the art of the sommelier

Rome's Rimessa Roscioli is a restaurant, wine bar, event space, and all-around shrine to Italian grapes. The restaurant's sommelier, Lindsay Gabbard, has a simple mission: to celebrate the wonders of Italian wine and the hard-won wisdom of those who make it. Roscioli's esteemed wine club has worked with over 600 artisanal producers across Italy in an effort to ensure that small wineries remain a central part of the country's story. The club seeks, in Gabbard's words, to connect "directly to the person behind the bottle." Italy might produce over five billion liters of wine every year, with some of the world's favorite grapes, but the industry is still largely dominated by small wineries—and it's these makers that Roscioli puts front and center.

Hailing from Detroit but now based in Rome, Gabbard trained extensively as a sommelier, but the most valuable experience came when traveling through Italy's vineyards. "So often, official classes don't talk about what matters to the winemakers themselves," she says, on a brief break from touring the wineries of Sicily. "Territories need saving and soils need replenishing. Visiting vineyards, touching soils, speaking to producers—that's the way to learn."

Gabbard fell in love with the sheer variety of Italian wine. "I love Italy's biodiversity. There are 800 or so grapes and endless flavors, endless traditions, endless landscapes—some that are vertical, some that are volcanic—with every single soil type." What about the country's best wine regions? Gabbard is understandably reluctant to pick only a few, but acquiesces: "Piedmont makes some of the most important wines in the world. Sardinian wines remain relatively unknown—those wines are wild." Beyond Vermentino, Sardinia's celebrated grape, many of the best Sardinian wines are still poured from unlabeled bottles near the vineyard itself, with no market beyond the island.

With so many wonderful grapes and such a vast tapestry of regions, it can be hard for the uninitiated to know where to start with Italian wine. That's where the sommelier comes in. "So many sommeliers use their role to show off," Gabbard says, "but you are there to elevate the visitor's experience and make the wine approachable. Your job is to be a bridge." And considering Italy has more artisanal winemakers than anywhere else in the world, there's no telling where that bridge might lead.

ICONIC WINES

Everyone's heard of Prosecco and Chianti, but what about Aglianico or Cannonau? Thanks to Italy's balmy climate and ribbons of vineyards, a whopping 545 grape varieties grow here, almost half of the 1,300 that are known around the entire world. Some are indigenous; others tell of Italy's history, brought over by ancient Greek, Phoenician, or Arab colonizers. Wine is a wonderful starting point for any Italian journey; wherever you go, the local grapes will induct you into the area, its culture, and its history.

Chianti, Tuscany
Made with predominantly Sangiovese grapes, Chianti is the most accessible of Tuscany's famous wines. The most prestigious varieties are produced in the hilly center of the region, Chianti Classico, which was first designated for wine growing by the Grand Duke of Tuscany in 1716.

Cannonau, Sardinia
Sardinia is known for its centenarian population, and this red, bursting with antioxidants, might be one of the reasons why. Grown across the island, it comes into its own at high altitudes.

Etna Rosso, Sicily
Mount Etna's volcanic terrain and seaside location makes for extraordinary wines that blend the fire of the volcano with a salty sea breeze. Planted on Etna's eastern flank, Nerello Mascalese grapes are the base for the surprisingly minerally Etna Rosso red.

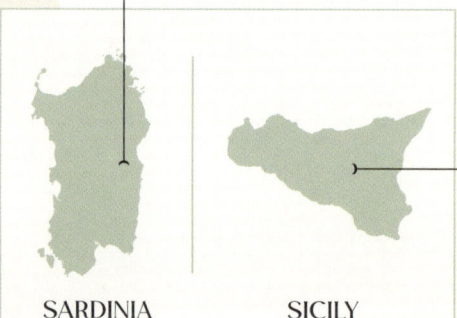

SARDINIA   SICILY

Prosecco, Veneto

Move over Champagne: the people's favorite sparkling wine is grown in the Veneto region around Conegliano and Valdobbiadene. The area is a UNESCO World Heritage Site home to terraced vineyards.

Barolo, Piedmont

The grande dame of Piedmont's fine wines, Barolo exploded on the global wine scene after a revolution in its production methods in the 1970s. Today, this full-bodied red is strictly produced from hillside-grown Nebbiolo grapes and is aged for at least 38 months.

Pecorino, Abruzzo

Little known outside of Italy, Pecorino is an ancient indigenous white, mostly grown down the Adriatic coast, from the Marche to Abruzzo. Straw-colored, mineral-heavy, and fresh, it's the perfect summer wine for a day on the beach.

Aglianico, Campania

As fiery as the volcanic environment it prefers, Aglianico is mostly found in Campania, around Avellino and Benevento. A full-bodied red wine, it's often known as the *Barolo del sud* (Barolo of the south) for its intense flavor.

DRINKING CULTURE

Putting the world to rights, drink in hand

A drink is never just a drink in Italy. It's a marker of time, a chance to connect with friends, even a way to signify to the body that it's time to eat. Stopping for a sip of something delicious is a daily ritual to be enjoyed, and meeting up at a bar—whether it's for a prework coffee or a post-work *aperitivo*—is not just a pastime but a habit across the country.

Sunrise ...

Gathering for the first coffee of the day—a shot of espresso—at a bar in major cities became an Italian social custom in the 1880s, with the patent of the espresso machine in Turin. Starting your day with a vital coffee fix isn't confined to Italy, but Italians sure took it to new heights, developing an entire morning ritual that's still held sacred. It's simple: stand at the café bar, order a coffee, maybe grab an accompanying *cornetto*, and enjoy them both while chatting with bar mates. The coffee ordered depends on the region, time of day and personal preference, but Italians tend to baulk at milk in the afternoon; ordering a cappuccino after 11 a.m. will result in an eye-rolling barista and chuckling locals. Latte art doesn't impress, in fact, lattes (and flat whites) are rare to find. And don't even think about ordering a cup to go; drink an espresso at the counter and nurse a cappuccino at the table.

... and sunset

Italians bookend their day with a glass of something special. If a coffee starts the morning and an *aperitivo* whets your appetite, then the *digestivo* concludes a meal and marks the end of the day.

Amaro, flavored distilled spirits that are drunk neat, are the most common type of *digestivo*, but they weren't always after-dinner drinks. They were first distilled by monks for their medicinal value, and the concoctions were made by infusing grape brandy with herbs, spices, and citrus peel. It was thought that drinking these bitter drinks after a meal would aid digestion, and so *digestivo* culture was born. The north has a strong *amaro* game, with the liqueur known to ease the harsh winter chill there, but every region, town, and many households distill a good *amaro*.

Not ready to call it a night? Stumbling upon a buzzing dive bar tucked down a quiet backstreet is one of the greatest parts of Italy's drinking culture. Pull up a chair, grab a glass of something good, and dive in.

COFFEE IN TRIESTE

Residents of Trieste—the capital of Italian coffee culture—are known to be the keenest observers of Italy's coffee rituals, and the city has its own language when it comes to ordering. Ask for a *capo in b* and you'll be served a large *caffè* macchiato in a glass, while a *gocciato* is a simple espresso with a small dash of steamed milk.

Clockwise from top left
A beautiful Venetian café; *grappa*, another classic *digestif*; taking a coffee break

WINE
WINDOWS

Spend enough time walking around Florence's grand *palazzi* and you'll begin to notice small holes in the walls. These are the city's utterly unique *buchette del vino* (literally "small wine holes"), with a history dating back to the 16th century. Large enough to fit a flask of booze and an arm to proffer it, they were a discreet way for noble families to sell surplus wine directly to customers. The privacy and security offered by these small windows took on a whole new meaning during the bubonic plague of 1630, when the windows were a crucial way for both buyers and sellers to avoid contagion. Since wine was thought to have medicinal properties, patrons would pop by the windows in the hope that a glass would heal them; they'd simply ring the bell, place money on a tray, and then be passed a flask of wine.

Today, there are thought to be more than 150 wine windows in central Florence, with more in the wider region of Tuscany. They fell into disuse over time, with many boarded up by the 20th century, but the COVID-19 pandemic saw some *buchette* unlocked once more. As Italy emerged from its first lockdown, an enterprising *gelateria* opened its *buchetta* to sell ice creams. Restaurants and bars with defunct wine windows on their premises followed, putting the windows on the map again for the first time since the Renaissance period. Ringing the bell is all it takes to revive this tradition. *Cin cin!*

> "Today, there are thought to be more than 150 wine windows in central Florence."

Left A glass of *vino* served through Vivoli's wine window in Florence

SOCIAL LIFE

■ ■ ■ ■ ■ ■ ■ ■ ■ ■

While we can talk big about Caravaggio and
the Colosseum, delicious food and natural
beauty, perhaps the real reason we love Italy
so much is the way that life is lived here. With
an onus on community, family, and daily
routines that never seem to get boring, Italian
life is as sweet as it gets and captures exactly
what *la dolce vita* is all about: enjoying life in
the present. It's why stopping to chat with
neighbors on the piazza; celebrating when
your favorite soccer team wins a match; or
choosing the ripest, reddest tomato you can
find at the market is so important to Italians.
And it's also why being in your 90s doesn't
stop you from walking miles every day or
thrashing your friends at a game of cards in
your local bar. Living life to the fullest isn't
about epic adventures; it's about the little
things, and that's how to live, the Italian way.

■ ■ ■ ■ ■ ■ ■ ■ ■ ■

THE FAMILY UNIT

Bonds that define Italian life

To say family is important in Italy is a striking understatement. Where you live, who you live with, what values you hold dear, even what meals you dish up at dinner—all of this is influenced and shaped by parents, grandparents, siblings, cousins, aunts, and uncles. Heck, it's even influenced by second cousins and aunts twice removed. Big, hospitable, and loving, the typical Italian family reminds us of the importance of community and connection—and what sums up *la dolce vita* more than that?

The extended family

To grow up Italian often means having your extended family close by at all times, learning to roll out pasta with your *nonna* (grandmother), and taking an evening *passeggiata* with your aunts and uncles. This might result in living in the same house as both your parents and grandparents, the same apartment building as your extended family, or, at the very least, the same town. Living with or near relatives promotes the close bonds, values, and traditions that are so tied up in family life, but it also comes with an economic bonus. With *nonna* next door, parents have extra hands for cooking, cleaning, and raising children, essential in a country without a national minimum wage, where both parents usually work. In return for this deep dedication to the family, children look after their parents in their old age, so much so that moving into a retirement or care home is rare.

For many Italians, there's an unwavering sense of obligation that roots them in their hometowns for life. Not wanting to miss birthdays,

Buon sangue non mente
Good blood doesn't lie

There's a guarantee that comes with a family name, especially in business, and some say that if parents are trustworthy, their children will be too. A sense of honor and good character is closely associated with the family in Italy.

family lunches, and life's big moments could mean not moving away—even for a better education, a more open-minded community, or a more successful career.

Of course, such a setup isn't true for every Italian family, particularly in more urban areas where smaller apartments don't allow for everyone and their uncle to live together. And while the nuclear family structure (father, mother, at least one child) has been the most common since ancient Rome, families aren't as big or as uniform as they once were, as many Italians embrace a life unlike the framed black-and-white photos at their grandparents' house.

■ ■ ■
Previous page A grandfather and grandchild **Clockwise from right** Together in the garden; father and son; the extended family

GRAZIELLA SABATINI

On the role of nonna in the Italian family

In the famously tight-knit network of the Italian family, one's *nonna* (grandmother) often sits proudly at the center—something Graziella Sabatini knows firsthand. Born in Rome in 1947, Sabatini now heads a large matriarchal family; with the help of her husband, she supports two daughters, her grandson Adriano, and her nephew and niece (whose young child is treated as a bonus granddaughter). Her extended family live close by, gathering for special occasions—Christmas dinners, Easter lunches— but also for school pickups and parties. Like many *nonnas*, she's there for both the big and the small moments.

"Grandparents are the heart of the family," she says from her home in Rome. "They're there to pass on love and provide a sense of belonging, security, and continuity." Though grandparents are highly important to families across Italy, Sabatini acknowledges regional differences. "In the south, grandparents remain fully integrated in daily family life. Remember, economically, things have changed: daycare used to be almost free, but now it's very expensive." The economic incentive for keeping *nonna* close *(p116)* is perhaps even more important in Italy's poorer southern regions. Monthly child benefit for many in Italy remains lower than in other European countries, just one reason why extended families, and particularly grand-parents, continue to play such a vital role. For Sabatini, caring for family never stopped her from working outside the home; all the women in the Sabatini family have juggled their jobs with domestic duties. A huge responsibility, no doubt, but Sabatini is eager to acknowledge that family time is always "about pleasure rather than obligation."

Sabatini also points out that the *nonna*'s role has changed in modern society, in spite of the many outdated stereotypes. "Grandparents used to be all toothless and hunched over. Now they are active—they even ride bicycles!" You only need to look at the huge number of sprightly octogenarians *(p136)* across Italy to see that becoming a grandparent no longer means sacrificing an active life. Things will continue to change both within and beyond the family, but Sabatini knows that some fundamentals will always endure. "Family is all about relationships, not just blood; it's about the love and support you build over time."

DIALECTS

Families and their wider communities are fused by the language they speak, which varies from one part of the country to the next and can be so different as to be mutually unintelligible. Say *"A quatt'e bastune"*—to be "on four walking sticks"—in Naples and locals will know you mean you're relaxed; in Tuscany, you might get a confused glance. There are around 200 specific dialects in total, all children of the Common Latin spoken in the Roman Empire, later influenced by centuries of geographical isolation, invasions, and cultural exchange. Here are just a few.

Ligurian

Ligurian gained a boost in the 20th century, thanks to the popular singer-songwriter Fabrizio de André. Most Italians might be familiar with *carrugi*, the name given to narrow Ligurian alleyways. *"Ecco che vieni nel mio carruggio!"* (Now you come into my *carruggio*!) is how Ligurians would say, "Now you understand me!"

Lombard

The Germanic Lombards who crossed the Alps ran roughshod over northwest Italy but adopted the local Latin dialect, leaving only a handful of mementos, such as the word for drink, *trincà*.

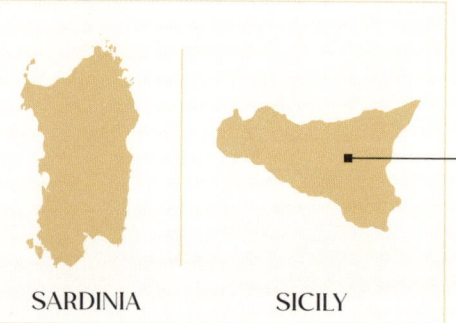

SARDINIA

SICILY

Sicilian

Sicilian is a mixture of languages such as Latin, Greek and Arabic, the latter of which contributed to words such as *azzizzari* (to beautify), from the Arabic aziz (darling). Notably, Sicilian has no future tense, which may (or may not) explain the island's famously laid-back culture.

Venetian

We have Venetian to thank for the Italian *ciao*, which derives from the Venetian greeting *s'ciào*, (literally, "I am your slave" but more akin to "at your service"). Shortened to ciao, it quickly spread all over Italy, losing its servile connotations.

Bolognese

The Bolognese term *umarell* describes the pan-Italian phenomenon of retired men who spend their time watching construction sites, typically with hands clasped behind their back, offering unwanted advice to the workers.

Florentine

Florentines have a habit of replacing hard Cs with aspirant Hs so that a simple sentence such as *una coca cola con una cannuccia* (a coca cola with a straw) is transformed into the Spanish-sounding *una hoha hola hon una hannuccia*.

Roman

Known for its rapid-fire delivery and colorful vocabulary, Roman was popularized through the work of Zerocalcare, Italy's most famous comics writer. Why not opt for a *bella zi* instead of a *ciao bella* to make a Roman smile?

Neapolitan

Nearly every Neapolitan will speak it, often more fluently than Italian. One of the few dialects with some cultural capital, it can be heard in the hit TV shows *Gomorrah* and *My Brilliant Friend*, often shown with subtitles for the benefit of those north of Vesuvius.

THE ART OF SOCIALIZING

Hanging out, the Italian way

Whether it's a quick and spontaneous conversation at a bar or a neighborhood gossip while passing through the piazza, community is at the center of daily life in Italy. Socializing underpins every aspect of the daily routine, from the first espresso to the evening *passeggiata*. On first visiting any Italian town or city, visitors might be struck by the extent to which social life is played out publicly—and, more often than not, loudly. Neighbors calling from terraced windows, genial retirees trading stories over café tables, and children playing on street corners—all of Italian life is here.

Forum to neighborhood

Social interaction, with an emphasis on the collective rather than the individual, is ingrained in Italy's infrastructure. The Romans designed many of Italy's towns and cities as fundamentally social spaces, with vast forums, intimate baths, and elaborate amphitheaters designed to facilitate communal living. Ancient architects like Vitruvius paid close attention to the design of the forum to ensure it encouraged public gatherings: Vitruvius stated that a public center should be big enough to accommodate a large crowd but not so large as to

overwhelm a smaller one. The Romans even invented the precursor to the apartment complex, with many citizens living cheek-by-jowl with their neighbors.

This logic extends to the cities and towns of today. Most areas are divided into smaller *quartiere*, or neighborhoods, with residents demonstrating fierce pride in their home streets. This is particularly true in the beautiful Tuscan city of Siena. Here, there are 17 distinct neighborhoods, each named after an animal or a color. Many of these neighborhoods are engaged in

THE STORY OF
Edicole (news kiosks)

Italian news kiosks *(edicole)* are more than just places to buy newspapers; they serve as hubs where locals gather to catch up on the latest neighborhood news and gossip. Engaging in a quick (or not so quick) chat at an *edicola* is a daily ritual for many Italians, even though they've now morphed into one-stop shops for tourists, too. Today, the family-run *edicole* sells public transportation tickets as well as toys, stationery, tourist guides, and local souvenirs.

Clockwise from left
Bonding over a game
of cards; stopping to
chat in the *quartiere*;
catching up over
gelato in Naples

INSPIRED BY ITALY
Social squares

The modern squares of today—Times Square, Trafalgar Square, and Red Square among them—mimic the layout of many Italian piazzas: large, open-air spaces where a statue or fountain serves as the focal point. Take London's Trafalgar Square, with Nelson's Column (which mirrors Trajan's Column in Rome) at the center. Along with this London square, Times Square in New York City and Red Square in Moscow serve as a gathering space and a place for events—there's little better than people-watching here.

La dolce vita
The sweet life

La dolce vita has become an iconic phrase, thanks to Federico Fellini's 1960 film of the same name, and is synonymous with the Italian way of life, where enjoyment, beauty, and living in the moment are valued. While the film depicted the decadent lifestyle of the Roman elite, today savoring a phone call with a friend or spending time with family all encapsulate *la dolce vita*.

friendly competition, with some "rivalries" dating back to the Middle Ages. The roots of any real enmity are lost to time, so the competition simply serves to enhance camaraderie.

It's rare for Italians not to know their immediate neighbors. These civic relationships are grounded in mutual respect: though Italy may like to live it up—with gatherings often lasting into the small hours—there are unwritten rules governing *buon vicinato* (good neighborhoods). These might include keeping the noise down after midnight and ensuring laundry is hung only in an agreed space.

Social cornerstones
Within the *quartiere* itself, there are a number of social hubs where Italians live out their public lives. The humble bar (whether in a major city or small town) is central, a vibrant community space where neighbors catch up, unwind, and enjoy each other's company. Here, a deck of cards might be cracked open and games such as *scopa* or *briscola* begun.

Away from the bar, this sense of togetherness extends to the *passeggiata*, or evening stroll. This isn't about reaching a destination— often the walk is circuitous, with no planned route—it's about savoring the journey itself. The walk might embody the Italian pastime of *dolce far niente*

(the art of doing nothing), but peel back the layers and you'll find that it's a fundamental means of maintaining a social network. Historically, the walk was a way for young people, dressed in their Sunday best, to scout out potential love matches, but nowadays the *passeggiata* includes the whole community. Take a stroll around Rome's dynamic Testaccio area to see the modern *passeggiata* in full effect: young revelers spill from bar to club or gig venue until the small hours.

Social cornerstones
That's not to say it's just the young that dominate Italy's communal spaces. Public scenes in Italy are often notable for the range of generations that mingle together, from young children to senior citizens. Socializing into your autumn years is seen as a highly important way of staying fit and healthy. The presence of older people in Italy's piazzas and bars is perhaps unsurprising, given almost a quarter of the country's population is over 65—the oldest average population in Europe. Many of these senior citizens stay actively engaged in their social circles, whether that's through morning meetings with friends or enjoying afternoons out with family. Life is structured around community, and that doesn't change with age.

...

Clockwise from top left Hanging out in Florence; a busy street in Milan; enjoying *aperitivo* at a bar in Rome

THE STORY OF
• • •

THE
PIAZZA

It all started, as things often do, with the Romans. As they conquered their way up Italy's boot, the conquerors graced each of their settlements with a large central forum: a town square where people would meet, shop, do business, worship, and conduct politics.

In the medieval period, the forum was largely forgotten by architects and urban planners, but Renaissance men and women took their lead from ancient Rome, and suddenly the forum was back. Only this time it was called a piazza.

Today, the piazza is the hub of any town. Some still have their original functions—like Verona's Piazza delle Erbe, home to a vegetable market that has been serving customers since ancient times. Others were built to show off political and religious power: think Venice's Piazza San Marco, which was conceived to be viewed from the sea; Milan's Piazza del Duomo, which draws all the focus to Italy's largest church; or Piazza del Campidoglio, Rome's political seat, which beckons visitors up a vast staircase to a mighty square (and was designed by Michelangelo, by the way). Perhaps the most perfect piazza of all is that of Pienza, in southern Tuscany, which was rebuilt from scratch by Pope Pius II as the *città ideale*, or ideal Renaissance city: the buildings of Church and State in a harmonious, perspective-led square.

Two thousand years from the days of the forum, Italy's *piazze* are still gathering places for locals and tourists alike. Some things never change.

> "Perhaps the most perfect piazza of all is that of Pienza, in southern Tuscany."

Left Piazza delle Erbe, once Verona's ancient Roman forum

127

MARKET CULTURE

A slower way to shop and socialize

If one were to describe the Italian way of living, it'd be all about slowing down and savoring the important things: that first morning coffee, the leisurely lunch with friends, time at the beach—and going to the market. Indeed, a trip to the *mercato* is an integral part of Italy's social fabric.

Growing together

Across much of the modern world, the supermarket reigns supreme. For many, shopping routines have been reduced to a frantic dart to the store, where plastic-wrapped vegetables with no discernible place of origin seem to exist in a state of constant ripeness, as if the seasons no longer exist. For lots of Italians, however, this model would seem completely alien. Particularly in smaller towns and rural villages but also across larger cities, an older and slower routine plays out, centered around the daily or weekly market. In larger towns and cities, markets might run seven days a week, while more rural locations have a dedicated market day. And there's nothing new about this routine: the ancient forum was long the setting for visiting market traders who sold the freshest local produce from the region.

Procuring the best produce at the farmers' market is a fundamentally social act. Market traders are closely linked to local farmers and producers, and they each have a wealth of knowledge about the season's produce. On weekends or busy days, regular market traders are often joined by small-scale farmers themselves, selling their own produce from the neighboring countryside and thereby ensuring continuity from farm to kitchen.

Wander any market and you'll overhear genial conversations between vendor and customer as home cooks source the freshest ingredients. A single glance at a market stall is a key indication of the season—and a means of remaining anchored to the natural calendar. In late spring, stalls burst with Sicilian strawberries as well as *agretti* (or monks' beard), fava beans, and peas, while summer sees an abundance of golden peaches and a huge crop of watermelons.

Vintage treasures

That sense of slowing down extends to fashion, too. In Italy, fast fashion is out, and secondhand is in. Vintage and antique markets—often laden with mid-century furniture, old crockery,

■ ■ ■ ■ ■ ■ ■ ■ ■ ■ ■ ■ ■ ■ ■ ■

AREZZO ANTIQUES FAIR

The Antiques Fair in Arezzo is the oldest and largest open-air market of its kind in Italy. Held on the first Sunday of the month, the fair is attended by some of the finest antiques traders in Italy.

■ ■ ■ ■ ■ ■ ■ ■ ■ ■ ■ ■ ■ ■ ■ ■

and racks of clothes—ensure once-loved products find new uses. There are an array of options when it comes to secondhand markets, including *mercati delle pulci* (flea markets, offering cheap clothes and bric-a-brac) and *mercati dell'antiquariato* (occasional antiques markets selling rarer, more expensive preloved goods). These markets provide a means for Italians to stay connected to trends of years past (which is to say they're the perfect place to pick up some '90s Versace or good-as-new Prada for a fraction of the price). Of course, this method of shopping is sustainable, too; with quality goods and clothes built to last, Italians rarely throw out the old to make way for the new. And when the clothes of yesteryear are this chic, who wouldn't want to bulk out their vintage wardrobe?

■ ■ ■

Above An antiques market in Bologna
Right A *venditore* (stallholder) with fresh produce

Clockwise from far left Fresh fruits and vegetables in Naples; artichoke for sale; street food vendors in Palermo; an antiques market in Bologna

WELLNESS AND WELL-BEING

Feeling good with the help of nature

There's an important phrase in Italy: *fare bella figura*. Essentially, it's all about keeping up appearances, looking good, and making a great first impression. But the phrase goes beyond vanity. It captures a more general sense of personal wellness, recognizing that feeling good on the inside means projecting a healthier image on the outside. Since time immemorial, *benessere* (wellness) has been an integral part of living your best life. And doing so naturally—whether that's bathing in hot springs, drinking herbal teas, or trying plant-based beauty treatments—is at the top of the list.

The Roman influence

Italy is a land of volcanoes, crater lakes, and thermal springs, and its earliest populations harnessed this seismic geology to its full potential. The early Etruscans bathed in hot springs, and the Romans took it further, making spa culture a key part of their social fabric. Lavish bathing complexes were built in every town, and baths were beautifully constructed, with a recognized spa itinerary leading bathers from freezing-cold pools to steaming-hot baths and everything in between. Two thousand years on, little—and sometimes nothing— has changed. At Cavascura on the island of Ischia, you can bathe in bathtubs whittled from the cliffs by the Romans, while at Saturnia in Tuscany, people bathe in the same volcanic lake that Roman soldiers used on their way home from battle.

Thermal culture

Subsequent cultures took their lead from the Romans, but the spa soon

---

■ ■ ■

Buona salute è la vera ricchezza

Good health is true wealth

There are a number of Italian proverbs that capture the central importance of a healthy life. This phrase suggests a healthy body and mind provides riches that far exceed material or monetary wealth.

■ ■ ■

THE STORY OF
Italy's herbal culture

Though most European countries offer popular herbal remedies, the market in Italy is among the fastest growing on the continent, with more than 50,000 herbal products available. Researchers are often startled by the perceived efficacy of many of these treatments. Studies have found that users across Italy feel considerably better after taking their remedy of choice, with a deep belief that nature knows best.

∎ ∎ ∎

Previous page Saturnia's thermal springs, heated by a volcano in Tuscany
Clockwise from top left The historic Santa Maria Novella Parafarmacia in Florence; Ischia's Sorgeto hot springs; hiking a forest trail in Emilia-Romagna

became an aspirational site used only by the rich and powerful. Through the Renaissance, princes and popes popularized the idea of hot springs as a place where the whole of high society could see and be seen. The idea took off, and lasted for centuries: author Mary Shelley was a regular to the Grand Duke of Tuscany's baths, now a hotel called Bagni di Pisa, and director Federico Fellini was such a fan that he set his film *8½* at the Chianciano thermal complex in southern Tuscany.

But you can't keep people away from a good thing, and today hot springs have been democratized once more. They are now considered so beneficial that Italians can be prescribed time at *le terme* by their national health system, while in (literal) hot spots such as Tuscany and Ischia, hot springs draw significant lines.

Nature takes the lead

That age-old recognition of nature's health-giving properties permeates Italian culture. *Parafarmacie,* as distinct from regular *farmacie,* are found all across the country, even in major hospitals, but they offer a range of herbal remedies alongside more conventional drugs. And while the Italian health system is one of Europe's most advanced, that doesn't stop doctors from prescribing the odd herbal tea or supplement. Perhaps they learned it from *nonna*—everyone has their own remedies, from locals on the Amalfi Coast who swear by lemons for every ailment to hay baths in the Dolomites, supposedly good for the joints.

Churches and monasteries, meanwhile, sell herbal remedies and toiletries made by monks, continuing the centuries-old tradition of botanical gardens. Historically, monasteries would appoint a dedicated monk as a herbalist; he would create various medicines from natural resources around the monastery. This wisdom laid the groundwork for later medical professionals, as early medical schools relied on the insights of Cistercian monks when writing their textbooks.

Out and about

But pills—even herbal ones—aren't the only answer in Italy. This is a country where wellness means raising the heart rate, often by exercising in Italy's extraordinary landscapes. In the countryside on a weekend? Whatever the region, you'll no doubt share the road with cyclists—solo bikers or groups out cycling Italy's beautiful, zigzagging roads. Perhaps the most popular cycling destination in Europe (sorry, France), it's welcoming to cyclists of all levels. Walking is also big here: the nightly *passeggiata* (stroll) around town is both a social act and a means of exercising pre- or post-dinner. Hiking in national and regional parks is also a popular activity, from the Cinque Terre coastal paths to the mountainous Parco Nazionale del Gran Paradiso.

Working to live

Though Italians are an active bunch, wellness certainly doesn't always mean pedaling up a hill. Sometimes, *dolce far niente*—the fine art of doing nothing—is just what the doctor ordered. Never is this more apparent than during the languorous summer months, when many businesses— including tourist-focused ones, such as restaurants and shops—shut down, often for the whole of August. Why make extra profit in tourist peak season when you could be a tourist yourself? Italians work to live, not the other way around.

BLUE ZONES

There's magic at play on the wild and sun-drenched island of Sardinia. In the leafy provinces of Barbagia, Ogliastra, and Nuoro, in particular, the number of centenarians is among the highest in the world. The island is one of the world's five original Blue Zones—regions where people live longer and healthier lives than the global average. The term was coined by American author and researcher Dan Buettner in 2005, and Sardinia was the first Blue Zone to be identified. Along with Icaria in Greece, the Nicoya Peninsula in Costa Rica, Loma Linda in California, and the Okinawa islands in Japan, these regions have been the subject of much attention over the last couple of decades for their unusually high quality and length of life. What's their secret? What these places all have in common is a diet of natural, locally sourced and mainly plant-based whole foods, regular physical activity, low stress, and plenty of quality time spent outdoors.

Family connections and local communities also play a huge part. Grandparents and elders have an active role within the family, which helps keep them engaged, purposeful, and well cared for. Many Sardinians still lead rural lives, hunting, fishing, and harvesting the food they eat, and walking several miles a day as they undertake their routines. Interestingly, Blue Zone living isn't all about deprivation. Sardinia's native Cannonau wine is rich in antioxidants, and drinking a glass (or two) a day is common. Whoever said staying healthy has to be a chore?

> "Many Sardinians still lead rural lives, hunting, fishing and harvesting the food they eat."

Left Enjoying life's autumn years

FESTIVALS AND EVENTS

A time-honored excuse to party

Italy's many festivals and celebrations are a common thread tying the country to its rich cultural heritage—and they also happen to be a great excuse for families and friends to come together for a good time. From those with an obvious religious connection like Christmas to obscure regional folk festivals and local carnivals like Lombardy's Grand Carnival of Crema, festivals and events are the highlights of the country's busy social calendar.

Celebrating saints

Given its Catholic heritage, Italy has a colorful panoply of saints, each tied to a particular region and with their own associated feast day. The patron saint day is considered a public holiday in a city or town, with businesses and schools usually closing to join in with the festivities. Sometimes, two Italian towns right next to each other have different patron saints, so one will shut up shop as the other runs business as usual.

The practice of commemorating significant figures on specific days has roots in the earlier Roman tradition of honoring gods. The Romans had a calendar filled with various religious observances, and this framework had an influence on how feast days were later organized in the Christian world. Central to these events was a hearty communal banquet, a tradition that lives on in the form of saints' feast days. These feast days were set on or near the dates of preexisting pagan festivals, helping along the transition from pagan to Christian observances in the 4th century CE.

Each feast day has its nuances, of course, but all involve some form of communal merriment. Take, for example, Florence's feast day for St. John (San Giovanni) on June 24. The day begins with a lively procession leading to the city's Baptistery, where a glowing array of candles are lit. In the afternoon, the 500-year-old game of *calcio storico* is played in the central square, a sort of Florentine precursor to soccer mixed with the rugged physicality of rugby. In the evening, fireworks are set off in the center, as families and friends gather to celebrate and give thanks. Across the country, feast days might be humbler or more extravagant, but the general principle remains the same.

A long Christmas

The Christmas season kicks off on December 8, the Day of the Immaculate Conception. Few

• • •

Clockwise from left
Carnival parade in
Crema, Lombardy;
Christmas night
on Via del Corso
in Rome; a Catholic
procession in
Nocera Terinese

BLOOD OF A SAINT

A curious miracle surrounds St. Januarius
(San Gennaro), patron saint of Naples. In
a crypt of the city's Duomo, a vial of the
saint's dried blood is said to liquefy
three times a year. It's seen as a bad
omen if the blood fails to liquefy.

Natale con i tuoi, Pasqua con chi vuoi

Christmas with your relatives, Easter with whoever

Even for nonreligious Italians, Christmas is still seen as the most important holiday of the year and, as tradition dictates, it's usually spent celebrating with family. Easter, on the other hand, particularly the Monday after Easter (*la pasquetta*), is often spent with friends.

countries do Christmas quite like the Italians, with a gloriously festive mix of tradition and modern decadence. First, decorations go up in homes and piazzas across the country, and huge Christmas trees are lit. Nativity scenes (*presèpi*) in churches and piazzas are also unveiled, a tradition that St. Francis of Assisi began in 1223 when he staged the first recreation of Jesus's birth using real-life participants.

Other countries might bring down their decorations and resume ordinary life come January, but not Italians. Building on the festive atmosphere of Christmas, the Epiphany, celebrated on January 6, is another national holiday and celebrations are very much a family affair. The day commemorates the moment when Christ was revealed to the world, symbolized by wise men visiting the newborn Jesus. The day is a time for tables full of traditional foods and the exchanging of gifts. Rome's Christmas market at Piazza Navona draws to a close on this day, and Befana (*p25*), often depicted as a witch, visits the square to hand out sweets to children.

Carnival and Easter

It's not long before the next major celebration: *Carnevale* (Carnival). The final festive event before Lent begins on Ash Wednesday; it is usually held in late February or early March. Across the country, masquerade balls, music,

parties, and playful pranks take place as people let loose before the 40 days of Lent, a period during which Catholics traditionally give up something like a favorite food or alcohol. The most iconic of these carnivals takes place in Venice, when revelers don elaborate masks—historically, this was so aristocrats could disguise themselves as they engaged in festive debauchery. Now it's just a chance to have a good time.

And then there's Easter. Instead of a bunny, in Italy you're more likely to find a dove-shaped cake (*colomba*), alongside plenty of chocolate eggs, of course. Each region observes its own special traditions, too. In Florence, *scoppio del carro*, or explosion of the cart, has taken place every Easter

THE STORY OF
Sagra degli Agrumi

One of Italy's most important spring festivals is the Citrus Festival, which takes place in Muravera, the center of Sardinia's citrus production. At the start of April, revelers welcome the start of the lemon season by donning traditional folk costumes as a parade of *etnotraccas* (decorated floats) passes through the streets, many depicting scenes from the island's colorful history.

Sunday for the last 350 years. It involves filling a decorative wagon with fireworks and leading it through the streets in front of the archbishop, who launches a small rocket (called a *colombina*, symbolizing the Holy Spirit) into the cart. As startling as it might sound, the more powerful the explosion, the better—the loud bang is said to bring luck.

Folk traditions

Not all of Italy's festivals are bound up with religion. In rural towns and villages, locals let loose at a host of folk festivals, many of which have origin stories stretching back hundreds of years. Every September, the mountain village of Cannalonga in the south of Italy hosts the Fiera della Frecagnola. This folk festival dates back to around 1450, when the festivities would coincide with a livestock market that brought quality meat to villagers. Today, the festival sees local musicians playing traditional songs and market vendors selling a host of local crafts. Perhaps the most beautiful of Italy's many folk festivals is the Infiorata, an

Italian tradition that dates back to the 13th century, when towns across Italy decorate their streets with flower patterns to welcome in the spring. The festival originated in Genzano di Roma, near Rome, and the town still hosts one of the best Infiorata displays.

Food festivals

It wouldn't be Italy without a calendar of food festivals. In ancient Rome, *sagre* were held to celebrate different

■ ■ ■

Above Patterns of petals at Infiorata, Syracuse
Left Christmas market in Vipiteno
Below Celebrating on the water at the Venice Carnival

gods and would end with an extravagant banquet for the public. These days, it's hard to find a town or village in Italy without its own *sagra*, and there are also plenty in major metropolises. While they're sometimes dedicated to the patron saint of the area, each *sagra* always celebrates a specific food or dish that is typical of the area. At the Sagra del Pesce (Fish Festival) in Liguria, heaped portions of delicious seafood are served from steaming vats as locals give thanks for the ocean's bounty, while in Piedmont, the annual Alba Truffle Festival sees a range of truffle-infused dishes served to hungry guests.

Political festivals

Though shared revelry is at the heart of Italy's favorite festivals, some commemorate serious historical or political events. On June2 , Festa della Repubblica is a national holiday that commemorates Italians voting in a national referendum of 1946; the vote led to the abolition of the monarchy and the establishment of a republic, paving the way for the Italy we know and love today. Celebrations in Rome center around the monument of Vittorio Emanuele II and Piazza Venezia, with large crowds forming to wave flags, watch the military parade, or simply to soak up the lively atmosphere. The highlight is the Frecce Tricolori, the Italian Air Force's jet team, which soars above the city, trailing green, red, and white smoke.

More recently, International Women's Day has become an important celebration of women's political solidarity. In Italy, it's customary to give a bunch of mimosas as a gift, the small yellow buds a symbol of female resilience. Groups takes to the streets on the

day to give thanks for historic achievements and to look ahead to a more equal future.

Cultural events

Though religious and historic festivals are still revered across Italy, the social calendar is also full of contemporary cultural events. Perhaps the biggest of all is the granddaddy of Italian music events and the longest-running TV music festival in the world, Sanremo Music Festival. Sanremo is held every February in Liguria, and was the basis and inspiration for the Eurovision Song Contest. Away from music, there's film. The Venice Film Festival is the oldest in the world and one of the most prestigious, held for the first time in 1932. Just as every saint has their day, so too does every art form, with a busy host of arts and literary festivals. In Italy, there's no cause too small for a party.

■ ■ ■

Above Celebrating International Women's Day in Rome

ERICA FIRPO

On the enduring importance of traditional festivals

The weight and influence of Italy's Catholic history is visible up and down the country: soaring cathedrals testify to the power of faith, while saint's days provide a living link to the past. But while faith continues to play an important role among some sections of society, Italy is becoming increasingly secular, with declining numbers of churchgoers—and particularly young churchgoers.

Why, then, do traditional events and festivals remain so prevalent across the country? Erica Firpo is a travel journalist, author, and podcaster, based in Rome. Though she and her family are not practicing Catholics, she has always been mesmerized by the spectacle of Italy's religious traditions and celebrations. "Italians really understand that you can celebrate a religious event with fun and with community spirit, whereas in some places these festivals forget the fun," she says. "Italians are able to keep the religious part without making it maudlin."

Her calendar, like many Italians', is full of traditional gatherings, from the *onomastica* (a name day in relation to the saint a person is named after) of her friends' children to large Easter lunches and extended Christmas parties.

Most weeks, it seems, there is another reason to bring people together. "This Sunday, in Rome, it's the Feast of the Immaculate Conception of the Virgin Mary, which is a holiday in the city. We have certain festivities: at seven in the morning, there's a procession with local firemen, who put a crown on top of a statue. Different bands come, and locals play music. Traditionally, the pope is supposed to walk from the Vatican to the main piazza—I love the ritual of it all." These events run the gamut from the grand to the gruesome. "There's always a macabre element to many of these traditions: you're often celebrating saints who have died. At the celebration of Santa Rosalia, for example, you see this woebegone figure carried on what look like four-poster beds—then there's the crown of thorns, of course."

Her extended list of gatherings brings home just how much these events mean to Italians, even those without a strong connection to the church. "I think these festivals are a great excuse to get together and enjoy a bombastic show. I love the pomp, circumstance, and spectacle, but mostly these are about celebrating with family." The number of devout Catholics may have fallen, but many traditions remain very much alive.

CELEBRATIONS

Across Italy's 20 regions, hardly a week goes by without a local celebration or religious festival. From patron saint days to centuries-old carnivals, not forgetting a plethora of food festivals, Italy has countless reasons to celebrate. Many of these traditional celebrations are specific not only to a region but to a certain town or village and have their own local rituals and delicacies to go with them. Here are a few of the best.

La Cavalcata Sarda, Sassari

On the last Sunday of May, the island of Sardinia convenes for a rich cultural celebration, when polyphonic folk singers create a soundtrack to hundreds of galloping horses, spectacular acrobatics, and traditional dances.

Truffle Festival, Alba

The tiny town of Alba in Piedmont is home to the International White Truffle Fair, famous for its truffle auctions and tastings. Throughout October and November, the festival showcases this prized ingredient, which can be found only in the forests around Alba.

Sanremo Music Festival

The inspiration for Eurovision, the Sanremo Music Festival, officially known as the Italian Song Contest, started in 1951 as a way of revitalizing the Ligurian coastal town. Held annually in February, it features artists from an array of genres.

SARDINIA   SICILY

Venice Carnival

Every February, Venice comes alive with a host of carnival parades featuring elaborate costumes and masks. The Lententide tradition goes back to the Middle Ages, but its heyday came in the 18th century. Today, sugar-dusted *galini*, *frittole*, and various other fried treats hit bakeries during the season.

Calcio Storico, Florence

Somewhere between rugby and soccer, this game started in the 15th century in Florence and is still played each summer between the city's four quarters. A stadium is set up in the grand Piazza Santa Croce, where residents and tourists lean from windows and balconies to get a glimpse of the action.

La Befana, Umbria

In the central regions, January 6 is dedicated to a witch called Befana *(p25)*—essentially Italy's own Santa Claus. The biggest celebrations are held in Urbania, thought to be Befana's hometown, over three days.

Grape Festival, Marino

The town of Marino—not far from Rome in the region of Lazio—hosts a prestigious *Sagra dell'Uva*, or grape festival, on the first Sunday of October. Go along to sample the new season's Marino DOC, a delicate and delicious white wine that's unique to the region.

Palio di Siena

Each July and August, the ancient Tuscan city of Siena hosts the Palio, a fiercely contested horse race held between 10 *contrade*, or city neighborhoods. Since the 17th century, the race has taken place around the Piazza del Campo, followed by a street party well into the night.

FERRAGOSTO

We all know that when in Rome, you do as the Romans do. But when *anywhere* in Italy in August, everyone does as the Romans *did.* In today's Italy, many locals take the entire month off work, with summer vacations peaking on August 15 for Ferragosto. This national holiday originates from the *Feriae Augusti,* a festival that was observed under Emperor Augustus, the founder of the Roman Empire. He instituted a day of rest on August 1, rewarding workers for their efforts in the lead-up to the harvest. That original, state-ordered R&R lives on today—*chiuso per ferie* ("closed for holidays") signs hang in shop windows, restaurants operate on reduced schedules or shutter completely, and offices enforce leave, with most people making for the beach.

A lot happened in between Emperor Augustus's reign and the advent of automated out-of-office emails. First, the celebration was moved to the 15th; during the early medieval period, the Church imposed a Catholic sensibility on the holiday, and Pope Sergius I transferred the date to the Feast of the Assumption. Centuries later, dictator Benito Mussolini built travel incentives into the day, introducing low-cost trains to curry favor with the working class.

Today, the relaxation rituals of Ferragosto are sacred. Though modern pressures mean fewer Italians can take the full month off from work than a few decades prior, it's still a near-given that people clock out for the week or two flanking the 15th, with the luckiest heading to family homes at the seaside or mountains.

> "A lot happened in between Augustus's reign and the advent of automated out-of-office emails."

Left Enjoying the waters of the coastal city of Cefalù, Sicily

THE SPORTING SPIRIT

The shared experience of a good game

It may seem trite to call sport a great social unifier, but in Italy, more often than not, it's absolutely the case. Watching or playing sports with friends and family is one of the most vital social experiences for so many, and the closest bonds are formed through friendly competition. Take a quick walk around any Italian village and you'll stumble upon kids knocking up a game of five-a-side on the piazza, soccer fans yelling at their team on a bar's TV, or retired folk playing the Italian game of *bocce*. Each is a small snapshot of sports' wider significance across the country.

Following unification in the 19th century, Italian patriots searched hopefully for *italianità*, a national quality that captured what it meant to be Italian. Just a century later, many claimed they'd found it: sports. Fascist leader Benito Mussolini saw its potential to unite the country and made it an integral part of his ideology, setting up the Fascist Academy of Physical Education—a kind of sports boarding school—in 1928. Even after World War II, sports remained a key political resource; it's no coincidence that former prime minister Silvio Berlusconi named his political party Forza Italia, after a soccer chant.

The beautiful game

In 1886, Edoardo Bosio returned to his hometown of Turin a changed man. He had gone to England to steal secrets of the Industrial Revolution, but what he brought back was far more valuable. When he organized the first "soccer" game among local factory workers, he was writing the first page in the history of Italy's national pastime. It wasn't long before the English game had become thoroughly Italianized, rechristened *calcio* ("kick," after the old *calcio storico fiorentino* game, a

THE STORY OF

Genoa CFC

Established in 1893, Genoa CFC is Italy's oldest soccer team. Founded as Genoa Cricket & Athletic Club by English expats, the team originally competed across athletics, with soccer one sport among many. But when the club won the inaugural Italian Football Championship in 1897, it quickly became one of the sport's dominant forces. The club won nine championships in total, with its last victory coming well over a century ago.

NOTABLE SOCCER MOMENTS

1400s
Florence develops the game of *calcio storico*.

1886
Edoardo Bosio organizes the first soccer game in Italy.

1934
Italy wins its first World Cup, winning another four years later.

1963
AC Milan becomes the first Italian club to win the European Cup.

1970s
Italian soccer hooligans bring about a violent decade.

2021
Italy beats England to win the postponed UEFA Euro 2020.

Previous page A game of soccer with a view **Clockwise from right** Winning the FIFA World Cup in 2006; preparing to roll the ball during a game of *bocce*; Ferruccio Lamborghini behind the wheel

loose medieval Italian precursor to soccer) and turned into a vehicle for national pride. After the establishment of local leagues and an embryonic national team, the country won back-to-back World Cups in 1934 and 1938, perhaps one of the first times the recently unified peninsula had managed to perceive itself as whole.

As Italy underwent a period of soul-searching after World War II, soccer offered a shared experience that helped obscure the country's political, social, and economic divisions. Fans gathered in stadiums and local bars to cheer on their local team, fostering a sense of community and belonging.

Of course, soccer has been at the heart of significant and sometimes ugly divisions in Italy. Club rivalries, like that between Juventus and Inter Milan, have been known to become

fractious and violent, while Serie A (the top league in Italian soccer) has been accused of corruption—accusations that reverberated throughout the political hierarchy. But this is all part of the wider theater of Italian soccer—it's no longer just a sport; it's a national symbol, akin to a new religion. Admired for its elegance and sophistication just as much as it's scolded for its corruption and melodrama, soccer runs deep.

Shooting hoops

It's not just soccer that brings Italians together. Basketball rivals soccer for popularity in many parts of Italy, and the national team is ranked as one of the best in Europe. One town—Porretta Terme, near Bologna—even has a church dedicated to it: the Chapel of the Basketball Players of the Madonna of the Bridge. Porretta Terme became basketball-obsessed after learning the game from American soldiers during World War II, and in the 1950s the town became the leading center of women's basketball in Italy. These days, Italian players, coaches, and fans come from all over to pray at the chapel, and the local priest has submitted a request to the Vatican to classify Madonna of the Bridge as the official patron saint of hoopers.

Playing fast and slow

But the social appeal of sports isn't always about high spirits and frenetic energy. While the English have bowls and the French *pétanque*, the Italians have *bocce*, a game associated with laid-back old men in villages smoking pipes and wearing flat caps. Like bowls, the object of the game is to roll your ball as close as possible to the *pallino* (little ball) on the other side of the court. Although it's largely

the reserve of the elderly in Italy, it maintains an importance among diaspora communities in the Americas, where it is seen as an integral part of their Italian heritage.

Sports in Italy represent both sides of *la dolce vita*: living slow like the *bocce* grandads, and the "live fast" mantra of the speed junkies who turned Italy into a pioneering force in Formula 1. Though France, Britain, and the US had a head start, it was the agricultural plains of Emilia-Romagna that emerged as the Shangri-la of motor racing. Many protagonists of the sport, such as Enzo Ferrari (*p172*) and Ferruccio Lamborghini, were from farming families and so grew up familiar with the mechanics of tractors and other heavy machinery. Together with Maserati, Ducati, and Pagani, they are all based in a small parcel of land between Bologna and Modena commonly known as *la terra dei motori*, the land of motors.

Winter sports

Soaring above these plains is a lush mountainous landscape home to Italy's winter sports culture. In some regions—such as Trentino—kids are practically born with skis on their feet, and hitting the slopes after school is routine in winter. Italy has taken part in every Winter Olympic Games, winning well over a hundred medals. A disproportionate number have come from the predominantly German-speaking Alto Adige province, among them Armin Zöggeler—"the Michael Jordan of luging"—who combined international success in the sport with his day job as a policeman. No matter where you go in Italy, watching or playing sports is all about passion, pride, and togetherness—little wonder Italians love a good game.

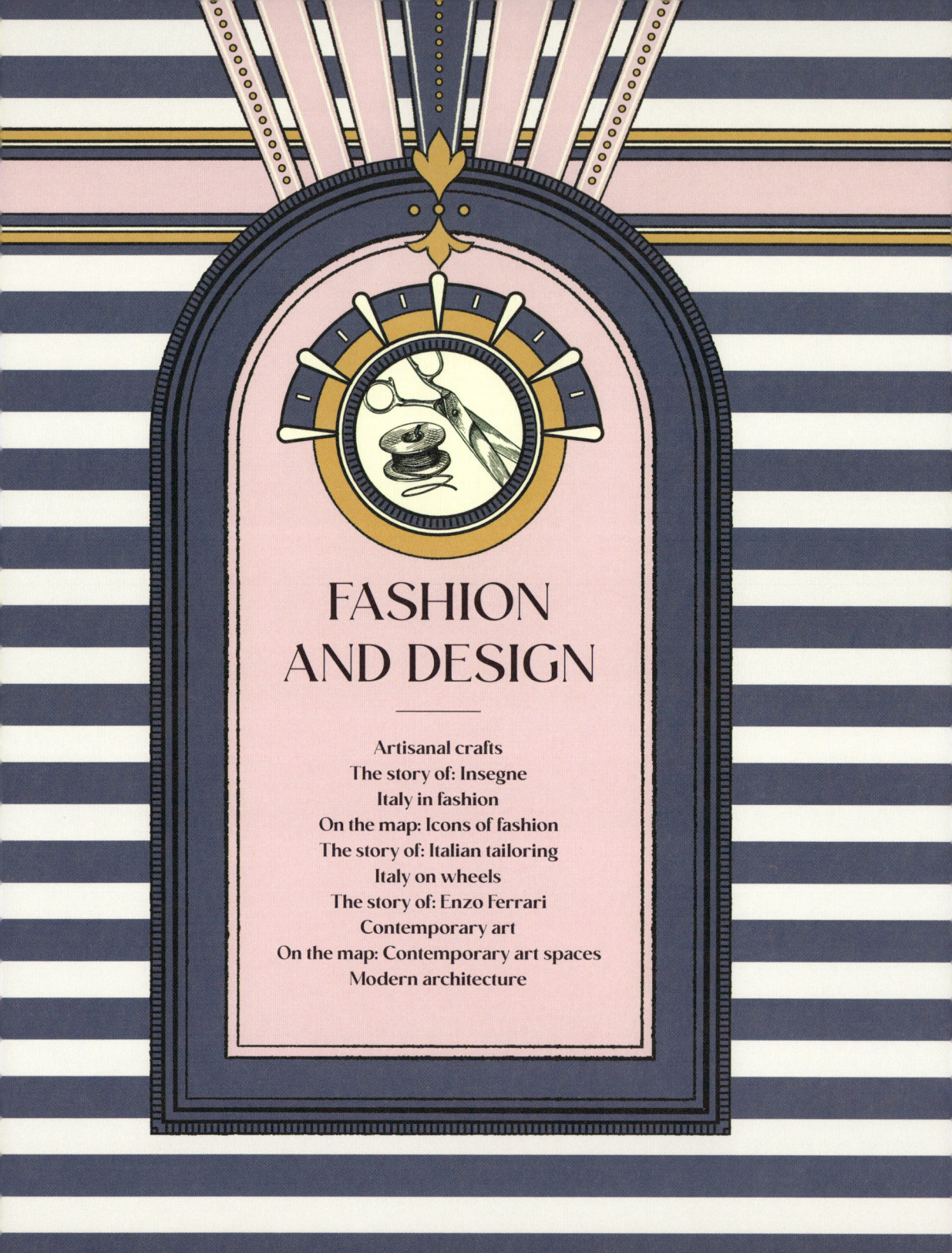

FASHION
AND DESIGN

||||||||||||||||||||||||||||||||

There's no denying it: Italy looks *good*. And
that's not just because of the beautiful
landscapes here. Over the centuries, Italians
have cultivated a style all their own—one that
the rest of the world can't resist adopting, and
why wouldn't they? After all, Italy has birthed
some of fashion's most beloved brands,
including Versace, Gucci, and Prada, and
created iconic pieces of clothing from Roman
gladiator sandals to exquisitely tailored suits.
But craftsmanship and impeccable design
isn't just in the clothes we wear; it extends to
everything here, be it the kaleidoscopic colors
of Murano glass, the stylish exotic cars of Enzo
Ferrari, or the dazzling contemporary
architecture of Renzo Piano. And while we
have Renaissance masters to thank for giving
us some of the world's best art, contemporary
Italian art isn't all cherubs and *chiaroscuro*;
it's bold and breathtakingly different, the
ultimate display of great craftsmanship.
Wherever you are in this beautiful country,
there'll be something to catch your eye.

||||||||||||||||||||||||||||||||

ARTISANAL CRAFTS

Centuries of history, crafted by hand

The gondola that guides you through Venice's waterways; the decorative pitcher on your restaurant table in Puglia; the leather jackets that locals sport around Florence—all have been handcrafted and are a representation of Italy's rich cultural heritage. Travel through any of Italy's 20 regions and you'll encounter storied artisans and innovators whose techniques have endured through the millennia.

A Florentine legacy

Italy's tradition of handicrafts dates back to antiquity, when the likes of shoemakers, goldsmiths, potters, and dyers made trade-worthy commodities. It wasn't until the Middle Ages, however, that artisans were formally recognized for their mastery, forming craft guilds (*arti*) to set the standards for craftsmanship. One of the biggest cities to be defined by these guilds was Florence, where they became an integral part of the city's society and economy. From the 12th century, the ruling Medicis poured wealth into these guilds to ensure the city maintained its reputation for Europe's best artisans. Each maker had its part of the city: goldsmiths hammered away in Santo Spirito (before being moved to the Ponte Vecchio), tanneries were confined to working along the Arno, and workshops were spread through the Oltrarno district.

Regional crafts

But while Florence was known as the city of quality and skill, nearly every region across Italy was perfecting its crafts. Murano, for example, is synonymous with glass. It's thanks to both *maestri vetrai* (master glass-makers) and an indefatigable guild that the tiny island held a monopoly on artisan glass and crystal creations. It also helps that the politicians of the Republic of Venice sequestered the *vetrai* to Murano in 1291 in order to keep their techniques secret from the rest of the known world.

The Aosta Valley, an Alpine region in northwestern Italy, meanwhile,

LE MARCHE

Anytime you put a pen to paper, think of Le Marche, where in the 13th century, artisans improved the craft of papermaking with the introduction of cotton rags. Papermakers in the town of Fabriano began weaving "designs" between the laid and chain lines of their loom to create unique watermarks.

has long been home to talented pine carpenters. The *grolla*, an intricately carved wooden chalice, is a beloved symbol of the region. North in Piedmont, Valenza has been the powerhouse of high-end jewelry manufacturing since the 19th century, specializing in delicate gold settings.

It's in the detail

By the Renaissance, craftsmanship began spilling over into art form. Several master sculptors of the 15th and 16th centuries began their training as apprentices in trades like gold- and metalworking, where they learned technique as well as the principles of design. Florence's acclaimed Lorenzo Ghiberti, who designed the bronze doors of the city's Baptistry, was one such sculptor, as was Donatello, whose bronze *David* would inspire Michelangelo to create his own masterpiece. This legacy continues today in the city, with local and international gold and silversmiths congregating in ateliers, creating designs that blend tradition and contemporary aesthetics.

A handcrafted home

Such artistic expression extends to homeware, too. Tuscany, Abruzzo, Umbria, and Sardinia have long been spinning the looms for fine wool used not just in high fashion textiles but folk art carpets and blankets, too. One of the most unique designs lies in Sardinia's *pibiones*, a weaving technique of geometric designs with a three-dimensional "pebble" effect.

Ceramics also go beyond mere decoration. Florence's iconic terra-cotta rooftops, for example, were created using a millennia-old tradition of crafting tiles that dates back to methods developed by the Etruscans. This is a nation where pride is stamped on every vase, glove, or rooftop and where artisans build upon generations of skill, tradition, and perfect artistry. In Italy, if it's not beautiful, it's not worth making.

||||||||
Above left Assissi embroidery, Umbria
Above right Alberto Conserotti, a master glassmaker in Venice

INSEGNE

Amid the bustle of ancient Rome's marketplaces, shops needed to stand out. Enter *insegne*, visual signs that indicated the service offered. In contrast to road signs (which were more formal and carved with Latin words), store signs used symbols (blacksmiths favored hammers; bakers, bread; and so on) to appeal to Rome's common people, who were largely illiterate.

Centuries later, store owners during the medieval period still used Roman-inspired motifs. Often hung from buildings or painted directly onto facades, the signs featured intricate carvings and bright colors to appeal to customers. Over time, *insegne* became art pieces in themselves, with elaborate designs and frescoes carved into ceramic and porcelain bases. Many Italian architects and artists played a significant role in enhancing the urban visual appeal during the Renaissance, and more change came in the late 19th and early 20th centuries, when the Art Nouveau movement swept through Europe. Flowing lines and elegant typography became favored designs, and cities like Milan and Turin embraced the style.

Today, Italy's urban centers often feature an exciting mix of traditional and contemporary styles. In Rome, the Via dei Fori Imperiali and the Roman Forum showcase remnants of ancient inscriptions, while the center of Turin is home to hundreds of examples of dynamic contemporary lettering.

> "Today, Italy's urban centers often feature an exciting mix of traditional and contemporary styles."

Left Modern lettering on Rome's Settimio Trattoria storefront

ITALY IN FASHION

More than just Milan

So much of what we know and love about fashion comes from Italy—luxury houses like Gucci and Prada, Milan's famous Fashion Week, a tailoring tradition that's second to none. From understatedly crisp Armani suits to saturated Pucci prints, the nation's style is wonderfully diverse and, naturally, grounded in quality craftsmanship and the pioneering vision of its designers.

The roots of the industry

Italy's penchant for fine dress might seem so chic as to be almost effortless, but fine minds have long been set upon perfecting a distinctive Italian style. In the 16th century, Italian courtier Baldassare Castiglione published *The Book of the Courtier*, a how-to text on what makes an ideal courtier. He coined the now well-known term "*sprezzatura*," a certain nonchalant attitude that makes whatever one does seem effortless. In short, he's talking about Italian gentlemen who make looking stylish easy.

Several decades prior to this book, Italy's textile industry was taking off. The Medici family's fortune, for one, was partially built on the textile trade, which, in turn, allowed artists of the Renaissance to thrive. The Medicis cultivated a perfect loop of creativity and wealth: the more art that was produced, the more refined Italian aesthetics became, the more people wanted fashionable goods made with the textiles the family manufactured. And so Italian finery came to be.

While the textile trade and the craftsmanship that grew alongside it formed the early foundations of Italy as a fashion capital, it took until the

--- ||||||| ---

La bella figura

The beautiful figure

Italians place a premium on *la bella figura*, but the translation doesn't cover it. A *bella figura* is less about putting your "best" foot forward and more about putting the "right" foot forward; it's about being appropriate for the occasion while bringing your own sparkle.

--- ||||||| ---

THE STORY OF
The "Made in Italy" label

Seen as a shorthand for quality, the "Made in Italy" label has been used since the 1980s to guarantee a product is designed, manufactured and packaged in Italy. Associated with fashion, the label is officially used across four industries known as the four As: *Abbigliamento* (clothes), *Agroalimentare* (food), *Arredamento* (furniture) and *Automobili* (vehicles).

20th century for others to catch on. The so-called "Italian economic miracle," a prosperous time that peaked in the early 1960s, gave rise to the glamorous image and attitude that we associate with Italians today. Just a decade prior to all the *dolce vita* excesses, the country was still reeling from World War II and largely reliant on an agrarian economy. Quickfire industrialization of the north, which produced iconic manufacturers like Fiat and Vespa, helped create wealth and demand for finely crafted luxury goods, of which fashion was up there.

At the same time, the Italian film industry was reaching its golden age and making its mark on fashion. Films like *Roman Holiday* (1953), which featured a coquettish Audrey Hepburn and a dapper Gregory Peck, and *La Dolce Vita* (1960), full of elegant looks, brought Italian glamour to audiences around the world.

The rise of fashion houses

The task of keeping these film stars stylish fell to Italy's great fashion houses like Prada and Gucci. It might be hard to imagine, but Italy's most iconic designers began life as humble family affairs. Guccio Gucci founded his namesake fashion house in Florence in 1921. He initially focused on making quality leather items, such as travel bags, using the time-honored techniques of Florentine leathersmiths. The founder's sons would continue to make handbags over the following decades, with their distinctive styles (bamboo handles, anyone?) catching the eye of stars like Elizabeth Taylor and Grace Kelly. The house's biggest moment came in the 1990s, when legendary designer Tom Ford took creative control, finessing Gucci's sleek, minimalist designs. He focused heavily on the brand's overarching image and perfected its presence on the runways, while honing Gucci's statement embellishments such as sequins, beads, and embroidery. The distinctive double-G logo became synonymous with Italian high fashion.

Prada also started in the early 20th century as a purveyor of fine leather goods. The brand's success is due

Previous page Italian elegance on display at a fashion show in Florence, 1959
Below Modeling Gucci's ready-to-wear collection for the 2024–2025 fall/winter season
Right top Showcasing style outside a Milan Fashion Week show
Right below Looking chic in Milan

largely to the founder's granddaughter, Miuccia Prada. A vocal advocate of women's rights in the 1970s, she worked tirelessly to perfect Prada's style, pioneering its signature light green hue, which became known as "Prada green." Under her leadership, Prada's cutting-edge designs and innovative fabrics would soon see the brand opening stores in London, Madrid, Tokyo, and Paris.

Epicenter of fashion

Prada remains indelibly associated with its stylish home city: Milan. Think of Italian fashion and you'll likely picture the busy Lombard capital, home to the now world-famous Quadrilatero shopping district. But while Florence's fashion scene was born out of its artisan guilds (p154), Milan would pursue a different

FIRST FASHION SHOW

Designer Giovanni Battista Giorgini hosted the first Italian high-fashion show in 1951 at his home, Villa Torrigiani, in Florence, a key moment in the industry.

one of the biggest events in the global calendar, and the perfect showcase for Milan-based designers, including Giorgio Armani and Gianni Versace. In spring and fall, all eyes in the fashion world turn toward the city.

Beyond brands

But Italian fashion hasn't always been confined to its grand brands, and by the 1970s and '80s, clothes didn't need a designer label to be deemed stylish. The practice of making fine clothes runs deep across Italy, and you're as likely to find style and quality at a small independent tailor—often run by the same family for decades—as you are at the country's best boutique stores selling ready-to-wear fashion. In this sense, despite the frenetic pace of the industry, very little has changed in the world of Italian fashion, and style, quality, and craft remain its renowned hallmarks.

The fashion world is changing far beyond Italy's borders, however, with an increasing onus on fast fashion and trend-based designs. From afar, it might seem that Italian designers will need to adapt to these new methods or risk becoming stuck with the styles of centuries past. Look closer, however, and you'll see that Italy's timeless chic and fashion's fickle trends have long coexisted. The future of Italian fashion, it seems, is about as black and white as your average Pucci or Missoni print—which is to say, not at all.

Above Giorgio Armani posing with models on the runway

route altogether into the heady world of high fashion.

In 1865, Luigi and Ferdinando Bocconi opened a store on the city's Via Santa Radegonda with a unique selling point: it sold ready-to-wear clothing. Customers could simply walk in and try on a suit jacket or pair of pants in a variety of sizes, without the need for a tailor. By the following year, the store was employing over a hundred workers to make ready-to-wear suits for men. The brothers would go on to open one of Italy's first department stores, Aux Villes d'Italie. Milan quickly made a name for itself not just by designing great clothes but by selling them in lavish concept stores—high fashion and successful commerce meant huge riches for this business-focused city.

In the 1950s, the National Chamber of Italian Fashion (Camera Nazionale della Moda Italiana)—formed to celebrate and protect Italian fashion and design—established the Milan Fashion Week in the city. It became

IN CONVERSATION WITH

ANGELA CAPUTI

⊢⊣⊢⊣⊢

On crafting beautiful jewelry in Florence

For over 50 years, Angela Caputi has handcrafted bespoke bijoux jewelry from her workshop near the storied Ponte Vecchio in Florence. The city has a long lineage of world-leading artisans *(p154)*, a legacy Caputi works tirelessly to keep alive. "The jewelers of Ponte Vecchio have a long history dating back to the end of the 16th century," she says from her workshop, which is housed in a grand 17th-century building. "Over many years, Florence's jewelers and goldsmiths have refined their skills and developed the best manufacturing techniques; I am proud that my creations are an expression of craftsmanship, not only are they 'Made in Italy' but truly 'Made in Florence.'"

Caputi's creations have been paraded on the runways of some of the world's finest fashion shows, but her jewelry has captured the world of fine art, too. You're as likely to find her striking necklaces or her geometric bracelets proudly displayed at Florence's Museo degli Argenti or Palazzo Pitti as you are on the catwalk.

But what inspires her pieces? "Each jewel is an expression of a state of mind or a feeling," she says. "I think that every woman, when she chooses one of my jewels, relives that state of mind in her own way." Though her styles and techniques are varied, Caputi is known for working with Italian-made synthetic resins, a material that enables her to achieve the vibrant colors and gentle geometric shapes for which she has become known. Each of her pieces is imbued with its own color and personality, a fact that has led esteemed movie and TV directors to seek out Caputi's jewelry when creating their characters. "I have always collaborated with costume designers for both Italian and global films and TV series. It's great to help them characterize a creation—there's a lot of work behind it, we can almost say a psychological study of the subject."

Looking ahead, she is keen to "keep the voice of craftsmanship alive" as she continues to innovate. "I started in 1975, when it was very difficult for a woman in Italy—not to mention a single one—to be able to create something successful that felt like her own; yet with strength, determination, passion, and many difficulties, I got here." Caputi has no plans to lay down her tools any time soon, with some of her finest creations still in the works. Florence's artisanal scene is in safe hands.

ICONS OF FASHION

Trends may come and go, but some elements of Italian fashion remain timeless. And they're timeless for a reason. Items such as gladiator saddles, *coppola* caps, and leather jackets have been designed and refined over centuries, and that's exactly what matters most to fashion-conscious Italians. Want to follow suit? Here are just a few staples from around the country.

Coppola, Sicily

When Michael Corleone hides out in Sicily in *The Godfather* (1972), he looks right at home wearing a *coppola*. These flat driving caps arrived here in the late 19th century via wealthy English visitors.

Prada handbag, Milan

Prada, Milan's iconic fashion house, debuted its nylon shoulder bags in the 1980s, but the brand has now updated its signature looks with the modern "re-nylon" range.

Leather jackets, Florence

Jackets are the coveted clothing souvenir for Florence visitors. The leather trade and tanneries were revived in the 20th century when one Guccio Gucci conquered the luxury luggage market.

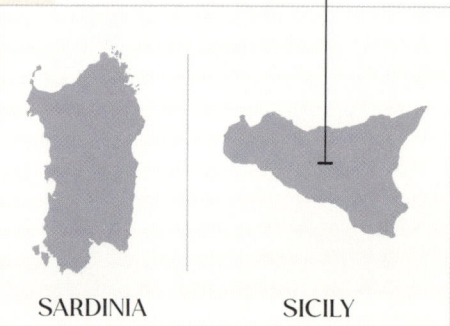

SARDINIA   SICILY

Velvet slippers, Friuli–Venezia Giulia

These snazzy slippers, also known as *friulane*, have a dandy air about them that belies their humble roots (they were made from scrap materials).

Felt hats, Trentino–Alto Adige

It's always function over fashion in this region, and the felted wool hat provides shelter from the harsh Alpine elements. Today, you're more likely to see gentlemen in wide-brimmed hats downtown than in the countryside.

"Soft-shoulder" suit jacket, Naples

If an Italian *gentiluomo* looks both buttoned-up and ultra-relaxed, you can probably thank his Neapolitan suit. With its unpadded shoulders and breathable fabric, this beloved staple is off-duty elegance at its best.

Capri pants, Capri

Though it was Sonja de Lennart, a German designer, who invented Capri pants in the late 1940s, it was the Italian island that inspired her. These cropped pants quickly garnered many famous fans in the 1950s.

Gladiator sandals, Rome

Whether lightly laced halfway up the leg or weighed down by chunky straps, Rome's gladiator sandals run the gamut from beachy-casual to avant-garde. They can be traced back to the ancient *caligae* worn by the Roman military.

ITALIAN TAILORING

As with so much of the country's creative output, the roots of Italy's famously impeccable tailoring—a craft closely associated with the *sartori* (master tailors) of Naples—date to the Renaissance, or roughly the 14th to 17th centuries. Alongside a robust textile trade, demand from the aristocracy for refined but not ostentatious clothing prompted the emergence of specialized tailors in cities. An early milestone was the 1351 foundation of Naples's *Confraternita dell'arte dei Giubbonai e Cositori* (Brotherhood of Jacket Makers and Tailors), which serviced European royalty and noblemen and is said to be the oldest tailoring association in Italy. The first generations began honing techniques that would be expanded upon in later years and, in some cases, codified to form strict laws governing the art of tailoring.

Not that these techniques emerged out of nowhere; tailors took many cues from the other titans of courtly gentlemen's style, the British. But over the centuries, and particularly in the 19th when Neapolitan tailoring came into its own, the Italian school distinguished itself from Anglo-Saxon stiffness in important ways: softer shoulders, lighter-weight fabrics, and ease-of-movement-minded silhouettes shaped by the Mediterranean climate. Today, demand for Neapolitan tailoring is beginning to outweigh the city's supply of trained *sartori*—it takes many decades to master the trade, after all. That effortless Italian style? It's one part mystery, two parts Mediterranean sunshine, three parts perfect stitching.

> "The Italian school distinguished itself from Anglo-Saxon stiffness in important ways."

Left A Neapolitan tailor at work

ITALY ON WHEELS

How Italy put art onto the autostrada

Italy's penchant for impeccable design isn't confined to the world of fashion. Leading automobile designers have ensured that Italian cars and scooters are never just modes of transportation; they're mechanical works of art. From Ferraris that skirt around Formula 1 circuits to Vespas that glide through Tuscan hill towns, vehicles have long been a representation of Italian style and freedom.

From Fiat to Ferrari

Italy's automobile revolution kicked off in the late 19th century with a little company called Fabbrica Italiana Automobili Torino—or, as we know it best, Fiat. Torinese businessman Giovanni Agnelli dreamed of propelling a newly unified Italy into the future, and for him, transportation would bring the country together physically as well as emotionally.

In 1899, Fiat was born, and the company started producing new economic cars in an assembly-line process similar to that of American car company Ford. By the early 1920s, Fiat was Italy's industrial and economic powerhouse, and its innovative Lingotto factory became Europe's manufacturing pioneer. Unlike anything else, the five-story building was a full-service factory for design, production, and testing on its rooftop track, and by 1936, Fiat wowed the country with its first car, the 500 Topolino.

Over in Emilia-Romagna, designers were less interested in the people's cars

"Il secondo è il primo dei perdenti."
"Second place is the first loser."

Variations of this quote are attributed to Enzo Ferrari. Throughout his long career, the designer captured his ruthless winning ethos with a number of these pithy sayings. He was endearingly brusque and endlessly quotable in interviews, summing up his storied career by saying: "I build engines and attach wheels to them."

and more focused on luxury sports motoring. In the 1920s, engineers and drivers like Enzo Ferrari (*p173*), the Maserati brothers, and eventually Ferruccio Lamborghini felt a need for speed and spent their time designing aerodynamic cars that set out to break records in the rallies and races around Europe. Bologna, Modena, Maranello, Imola, and the surrounding area soon emerged as Motor Valley, a hub of high-performance car and motorcycle production that included some of the world's most iconic automotive brands: Ferrari, Lamborghini, Maserati, Ducati, Dallara, Pagani, and the like. High-horsepower engines, coupled with beautifully angular designs, made these some of the most iconic vehicles in the world.

Everyday transportation

Beauty and speed couldn't overtake the requirement for practicality, however, and in the wake of World War II, the country was more in need of affordable transportation than ever.

||||||||||
Top A proud Fiat 500 owner posing by his new vehicle
Above The slick Maserati GT 2000 Alemanno, produced in 1956

NOTABLE ITALIAN VEHICLES

1936
Fiat Topolino, one of the world's smallest cars, launches.

1947
The 125 S, Ferrari's first car, debuts at the Piacenza racing circuit.

1957
Launched as a successor to the Topolino and Fiat 600, the Nuova 500 hits the streets.

1967
Known as the Daytona, the Ferrari 365 GTB/4 debuts with much fanfare.

1968
The brand-new Vespa Primavera embodies the freedom of Italy's youth culture.

1980
The boxy Fiat Panda is unveiled as Italy's utility car. Production ends in 2003.

2015
Motorsport's first woman CEO, Livia Cevolini, launches the electric motorcycle, the Energica Ego.

Clockwise from top left Driving a scooter through the narrow streets of Bari, Puglia; Ferrari 458 Italia roaring through Piazza della Scala in Milan; Audrey Hepburn riding a Vespa in *Roman Holiday*; a Ferrari 250 GT Europa, an iconic vintage sports car

Pagani Supercar

When Horacio Pagani was a small boy in Argentina, he dreamed of designing racing cars like those from Italy. Cut to 1992, and Pagani launched Pagani Automobili, producer of the world's most exclusive hypercars. Hand constructed in Modena, the Pagani Zonda and Huayra are renowned for their craftsmanship.

Innovation continues

Beauty, speed, and usability are all still important in Italy, but the nation is now leading in another field: sustainability. Manufacturers in Motor Valley are championing locally sourced as well as recycled and regenerated materials like carbon fiber, as well as leaning more on handcrafted automobile production. Energica led the charge in 2015 with the Energica Ego, the world's first high-performance electric motorcycle. They were quickly followed by companies like Pininfarina, who designed rapid sustainable supercars, and new start-ups like Aehra, who seek to prove that Italy can be the new home of sustainable luxury cars. By 2026, Ferrari will join the revolution with its first fully electric vehicle going on sale, signaling a new era of innovation for this beloved brand, without sacrificing speed and luxury. As Enzo Ferrari himself often said, "the best Ferrari is always the next one."

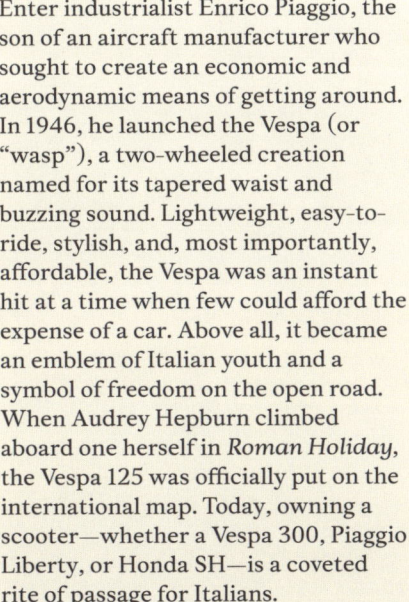

Enter industrialist Enrico Piaggio, the son of an aircraft manufacturer who sought to create an economic and aerodynamic means of getting around. In 1946, he launched the Vespa (or "wasp"), a two-wheeled creation named for its tapered waist and buzzing sound. Lightweight, easy-to-ride, stylish, and, most importantly, affordable, the Vespa was an instant hit at a time when few could afford the expense of a car. Above all, it became an emblem of Italian youth and a symbol of freedom on the open road. When Audrey Hepburn climbed aboard one herself in *Roman Holiday*, the Vespa 125 was officially put on the international map. Today, owning a scooter—whether a Vespa 300, Piaggio Liberty, or Honda SH—is a coveted rite of passage for Italians.

ENZO FERRARI

There are few figures in the world of global motorsport as revered as *Il Commandatore*, Enzo Ferrari (1898–1988). Born in Modena, Ferrari became captivated by the mechanics of fast cars while helping in his father's garage. As his peers were playing soccer or studying for exams, Ferrari was puzzling over alternators and cooling systems. In 1919, he secured his first job in the industry, working with the manufacturer Costruzioni Meccaniche Nazionali in Turin, first as a tester then as a race driver. Ferrari's early success on the track would later give him a winning edge over his business rivals—he understood the high-octane world of motor racing, both on the circuit and among the oil and grease of a workshop.

He soon began a collaboration with Alfa Romeo, where he founded his racing team, Scuderia Ferrari, who would adopt the most iconic logo in the world of luxury automobiles: the prancing horse. It wasn't long before Ferrari and his team were designing their own cars, starting with the legendary 125 S in 1947. The vehicle—only two of which were ever made—had many of the hallmarks of the Ferraris we know and love today: a sleek body, a ferocious V-12 engine, and that distinctive shade of red. Within three years, the team were racing in Formula 1, and they would compete in every championship after 1950, winning over 200. Off the track, Ferrari's entrepreneurial spirit saw him turn his company into one of the most exclusive brands. He may have died in 1988, but the prancing horse lives on as a universal (and oh so stylish) symbol of motoring success.

> "There are few figures in the world of global motorsport as revered."

Left Enzo Ferrari in his 40–60 HP Alfa Romeo 1920

CONTEMPORARY ART

Breathing new life into Italy's artistic landscape

When we think about Italy's artistic contributions to the world, we tend to look back to the Renaissance and Baroque periods, where masters and masterpieces were everywhere. But to limit Italy's artistic output to centuries past is to miss a key part of the country's creative story. From postwar experiments in conceptualism to a vibrant street-art scene, contemporary artists have influenced conversations in art, identity, and politics, just like Raphael and Leonardo before them.

Futurism forward

Italy's contemporary artistic scene began to establish itself during the social and political tumult of the early 20th century. The century kicked off with a bang in 1909, when Italian writer Filippo Tommaso Marinetti published *Futurist Manifesto*. The book launched a social, artistic, and architectural *(p182)* movement that sought to shake off the past in favor of innovation, technology, and speed. Marinetti saw the weight of the past as oppressive and was soon joined in his opinion by the likes of Giacomo Balla, Gino Severini, and Umberto Boccioni. Around World War I, the Futurists glorified a hyper-masculine world of engines and war machines, with technology framed as the aggressive force driving humanity into the future. If just one piece exemplified what Futurism meant in the art world, it would be Boccioni's striking *Unique Forms of Continuity in Space* (1913), an unusual humanoid sculpture frozen in dynamic motion. The armless and faceless figure is all fluid lines and curves so that it seems a strange hybrid of man and machine. This would mark the high point of Futurism, before two world wars changed Italian art forever.

Pushing boundaries

Grappling with economic, emotional, and artistic devastation following World War II, artists turned away from the aggressive, technological world view of the Futurists to explore new political and metaphysical themes in a changed world.

Perhaps the most radical postwar movement was Arte Povera, which emerged in the 1960s to challenge notions of value and commodification. Literally meaning "poor art," Arte Povera saw artists use everyday materials (wood, rags, soil, and even trash) in cynical, satirical, and

"""""""

Clockwise from left
*Unique Forms of
Continuity in Space;
Venus of the Rags*
installation; one of
Marinetti's visual
art pieces

"One movement has always prompted the radical response of another."

Just as the developments of the Renaissance inspired the Baroque, one movement has always prompted the radical response of another. By the 1970s, the daring artists of the new Transvanguardia movement responded to the alleged cynicism of Arte Povera by turning away from conceptual art. Not everyone agreed that rejecting the past meant rejecting the fun of visual art, so artists like Sandro Chia, Francesco Clemente, and Enzo Cucchi produced mesmerizing paintings exploring human identity. Clemente's *The Fourteen Stations* (1980) merged religious symbolism with abstract forms and vibrant colors. Sandro Chia created huge canvases like *Most Ghost Post* (1987), each loaded with vibrant colors and shapes creating a lively dream world. His large works were a refreshing reminder of the joys of painting.

To the future

As the 20th century came to a close, a host of new technologies and media opened up entirely fresh forms of visual art. Artist Vanessa Beecroft started to create "living pictures" through performance art. Her video tableau *VB01* (1993) featured 30 near-motionless women all sharing the artist's "Book of Food," a diary

Left Sando Chia's dynamic oil painting, *Most Ghost Post*
Right Italian artist Francesco Clemente, a key figure of the Transvanguardia movement

often absurd ways to disrupt the commercialized art industry. Lucio Fontana's *Spatial Concept: Waiting* (1958), a white canvas with vertical cuts, ripped apart the elite world of fine art, while Michelangelo Pistoletto cleverly continued the rebellion with *Venus of the Rags* (1967/2023), a series of installations that saw prized sculptures set alongside towering piles of soiled rags. Perhaps the most iconic moment of all came when Piero Manzoni created *Artist's Shit* (1961). The piece comprised 90 tin cans, each (supposedly) containing the artist's own excrement. Like great works of art, each tin was valued at the price of gold.

documenting Beecroft's struggle with bulimia.

Artists got ever bolder as the decades progressed and the boundaries of artistic taste shifted. One such artist was Maurizio Cattelan. Known as the satirical bad boy of the Italian art scene, his artwork dares you to question the bleak reality of the modern world (while laughing at it at the same time). His provocative sculpture *L.O.V.E.* (2010), a huge middle finger and literal "F*** Off" to Milan's stock exchange, is a case in point. Fittingly, the sculpture sits in the heart of Milan's banking sector.

Perhaps the biggest form of social commentary, however, came from artists taking to the streets in the 21st century. Mark-making has been fundamental to the Italian art scene since the very first *graffito* daubed

the walls of ancient Rome, and today, many of Italy's cities are canvases for some of the world's best street artists. There's no entrance fee, no rules, and no boundaries when it comes to enjoying the work of OZMO, a Milanese artist who recycles High Renaissance imagery, and Alicè (Alice Pasquini), who creates larger-than-life figurative murals and small stencils exploring relationships, emotions, and femininity. No matter what decade and genre, Italy's contemporary art scene thrives because it both leans on its historical mastery while looking beyond it. There will forever be a place for Michelangelo and Caravaggio in Italy's canon, but as long as there's a gallery wall or side street to work on, new artists with a dream will continue to give these old masters a run for their money.

Above Maurizio Cattelan's *L.O.V.E.* in Milan's Piazza degli Affari

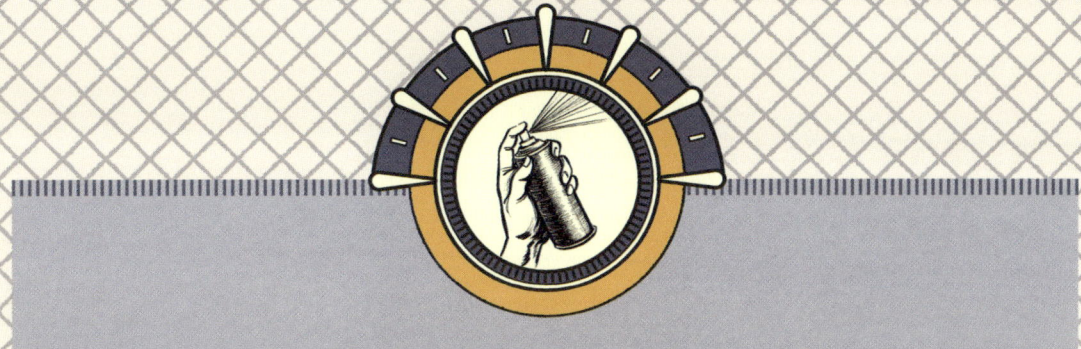

IN CONVERSATION WITH

ALICE PASQUINI

—— ||||| ——

On the thriving world of Italian street art

"I started to paint on the street because I was feeling repressed by the idea of art in Italy," says esteemed street artist Alice Pasquini from her base in Rome. For a young Italian artist, the shadow of the country's celebrated masters looms large; this is the country of Leonardo and Michelangelo, after all—artists who irrevocably shaped the institution of Western art. Seeking liberation from the stifling world of the classical gallery, Pasquini took her talents to the streets. "Graffiti arrived to me at a perfect moment. It set me free from the academy," she says.

Street art is not new in Italy, of course—vibrant tags across the streets of Pompeii attest to the fact that artists have been pasting their creativity on walls since the days of ancient Rome. But these days, artists like Pasquini are forging ahead with a new artistic tradition, one which remains fundamentally democratic. She began spraying small murals in the Italian capital, but her work is now to be found on walls and canvases in over 100 cities around the world.

For Pasquini, street art is best when it's sensitively integrated into its surroundings. This is both technical—using "the background, the shape, and color of the wall"—but also cultural, with works capturing the nuances of a community. "I feel a deep responsibility when I paint outside: who will see this? Who will be looking at this every day? I think about the culture and the religion of the place." Few projects capture Pasquini's ethos quite like the festival she founded, CVTà Street Fest. Back in 2014, Pasquini received an invitation to paint the village of Civitacampomarano, which happened to be where her grandfather had lived. Upon returning to the village where she'd spent her childhood summers, she found a crumbling place ravaged by depopulation; residents had fled en masse due to a lack of opportunity. So she did what she does best, enlisting friends and locals to daub small murals and paintings.

Cut to a decade later, and these efforts have regenerated Civitacampomarano, with new residents arriving and old faces returning. The first Street Fest was held here in 2016, and it has been running yearly since, the work of artists and local volunteers. "The village is living again," says Pasquini, as she looks ahead to the festival's next iteration. "This is both a personal and a collective story. Street art becomes important through the people, and that is its power."

CONTEMPORARY ART SPACES

We all know and love the Uffizi and Vatican Museums, but Italy's gallery scene doesn't end there. Blockbuster national galleries like Rome's La Galleria Nazionale remain the backbone of Italy's art scene, but it's pioneering galleries such as Naples's Galleria Lia Rumma, world-renowned events like the Venice Biennale, and amazing spaces including Rome's MAXXI that continue to push Italy's contemporary creativity.

Fondazione Sandretto Re Rebaudengo, Turin

Home to the collection of Italy's most eminent contemporary art collector, Patrizia Sandretto Re Rebaudengo, this foundation showcases an array of blockbuster exhibitions.

Fondazione Prada, Milan

This is the brainchild of fashion designer Miuccia Prada and her husband Patrizio Bertelli, and it's a fashionable space in itself. A former gin distillery turned cutting-edge compound, the multispace foundation always features a lineup of provocative shows alongside its permanent collection.

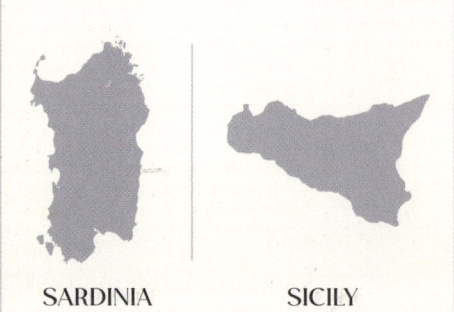

SARDINIA

SICILY

Pinacoteca Agnelli, Turin

Creators of Fiat, the Agnelli family have an excellent art collection, which is housed on the top floor of their former car factory. You'll find art dating from between the 18th and 20th centuries here.

Venice Biennale

One of the most prestigious art exhibitions in the world, the Biennale is spread across two areas: the Giardini della Biennale and the Arsenale, which hosts large group shows.

Galleria Continua, San Gimignano

Lorenzo Fiaschi's flagship gallery stands as one of Italy's most prestigious art spaces, featuring works by icons like Daniel Buren, Antony Gormley, and Mona Hatoum.

La Galleria Nazionale, Rome

A few steps from the Villa Borghese park is a Neo-Classical palace hosting Italy's national collection of modern and contemporary art, curated non-chronologically.

Galleria Lia Rumma, Naples

Founded in 1971, this gallery has launched the careers of art-world giants like Joseph Kosuth and Mimmo Jodice, while introducing Italian audiences to international stars like Marina Abramović.

MAXXI, Rome

This iconic, futuristic space was designed by Zaha Hadid in 2009. It put Rome firmly on the contemporary arts map, with a collection that's entirely focused on 21st-century art.

MODERN ARCHITECTURE

Building for the future

Following the 1870 unification of Italy, the country needed something ... new. Stripping away the flourishes of their forebears, modern architects boldly built for the country's future. But the weight of such an incredible architectural legacy hasn't been easy to ignore. Today, contemporary architects are tasked with creating modern structures that honor the country's past while pushing the boundaries of innovation. It's no easy feat, but it makes for some dazzling panoramas.

Moving with Modernism

As the 20th century dawned, architects looked toward new materials to carry them into the modern age. With new technologies (and a good deal of concrete), Modernism was born. Clean lines, industrial aesthetics, and minimalist designs swept through Italy. Perhaps the most famous example of this movement was the Fiat Lingotto factory in Turin. Designed by Giacomo Mattè-Truccio, this 1,640 ft (500 m) long rectangular building acted as the car company's factory and headquarters. Its hulking mass of strong reinforced concrete was a formidable sight, but its crown jewel was the

0.5-mile (1 km) rooftop racetrack where Fiat could test cars made in the factory below. An icon of Modernism, it was praised by famous architects such as Le Corbusier and even featured in *The Italian Job* (1969).

As the Modernist movement continued to gain traction across Europe in the 20th century, Italian architects soon developed their own version of the style. Spearheaded by a group known as the Gruppo 7, *Razionalismo* (Rationalism) combined the Neo-Classical excess of ancient Rome with the bold angles of Futurism to create a new image of modern Italy. The aggressively confident movement was linked to the Fascist ideologies at play during the time and was closely supported by Fascist leader Benito Mussolini, who financed numerous projects. Buildings such as the Casa del Fascio (the former office of the National Fascist Party in Como) and the EUR district in Rome (an area of wide boulevards and columned buildings) are clear examples of Fascist ideals in architectural form.

Postwar modern living

The end of World War II heralded a new era for Italy's architecture. Cities were in ruins, and architects had a

NOTABLE ITALIAN ARCHITECTURE

1916–1923
Giacomo Mattè-Trucco designs the Fiat Lingotto, a vast car factory with a track on the roof, in Turin.

1937–1942
Giovanni Guerrini, Ernesto Bruno La Padula, and Mario Romano design the Fascist-era Colosseo Quadrato and EUR district in Rome.

1930
La Città Metafisica in Tresigallo is created to serve as a Utopian city.

1938–1940
Architect Adalberto Libera creates the Modernist Casa Malaparte in Capri.

social responsibility to rebuild. As a result, numerous housing projects rose from the ashes, putting functionality at the forefront as they aimed to address urban poverty. Yet the devastation also sparked a renaissance in experimentation. Ruined cities became a blank canvas, spurring architects to reimagine living spaces for a new postwar world. Architects like Gio Ponti, who created Milan's iconic Pirelli Tower, rose to prominence with their innovative use of materials and love of glass. Others, such as Carlo Scarpa, took experimentation to the max; Scarpa's formidable Brion Cemetery looks so futuristic (even today) that it was used as a location for *Dune: Part Two* (2024).

An international age

Italian architecture reached new heights during the 1990s and early 2000s, thanks to an influx of national and international starchitects—with the budget to match their extraordinary visions. They created buildings entirely at odds with our romantic vision of Italy as a place of pretty churches and colosseums. Italian-born Renzo Piano led the way with groundbreaking designs like Rome's Parco della Musica (1994–2002) and Maranello's Ferrari Wind Tunnel (1997), structures so futuristic it was as if Italy had time-warped.

Meanwhile, American architect Richard Meier created the Church of the Jubilee (2003) in Rome, its three nestled sails reaching up to the heavens, and Iraqi-British architect Zaha Hadid designed the MAXXI Museum (2010) in Rome, a sinuous sprawl of concrete.

A sustainable future

Just as car manufacturers and fashion designers were thinking of sustainable new designs, architects began to incorporate eco-friendly elements into their work in the 21st century. The vertical forests of Stefano Boeri's Bosco Verticale (2014), a midsize skyscraper with over 20,000 plants rooted in the building's structure, is easily Italy's most famous example of this. Architects such as Santiago Calatrava have designed striking new transport hubs like Reggio Emilia's main station, a gesture of commitment to the future of sustainable travel.

Today, more architects are looking to reinterpret existing spaces as they push Italian innovation forward. Pioneers of the future, like Milanese firm LPzR, design buildings that facilitate social communal living. While their designs might be new, their communal ethos is perhaps a throwback to those vast ancient plazas—just another way in which Italy preserves the past as it looks to the future.

ıııııııııı

Previous page Rome's Colosseo Quadrato, also known as the Square Colosseum **Clockwise from top left** Bosco Verticale, Milan; Reggio Emilia's wavy roof; Church of the Jubilee, Rome

1932–1935	1955–1958	1955–1960	1968–1978	2009–2014
Milanese Rationalist architect Piero Portaluppi designs Milan's Villa Necchi Campiglio.	Firm BBPR shifts the needle with the build of the skyscraper Torre Velasca in Milan.	Gio Ponti and Pier Luigi Nervi design Milan's Pirelli Tower, a 32-story skyscraper.	Carlo Scarpa creates the Brion Cemetery, a modern wonder, in San Vito d'Altivole.	Stefano Boeri's sustainable masterwork, Bosco Verticale, graces Milan.

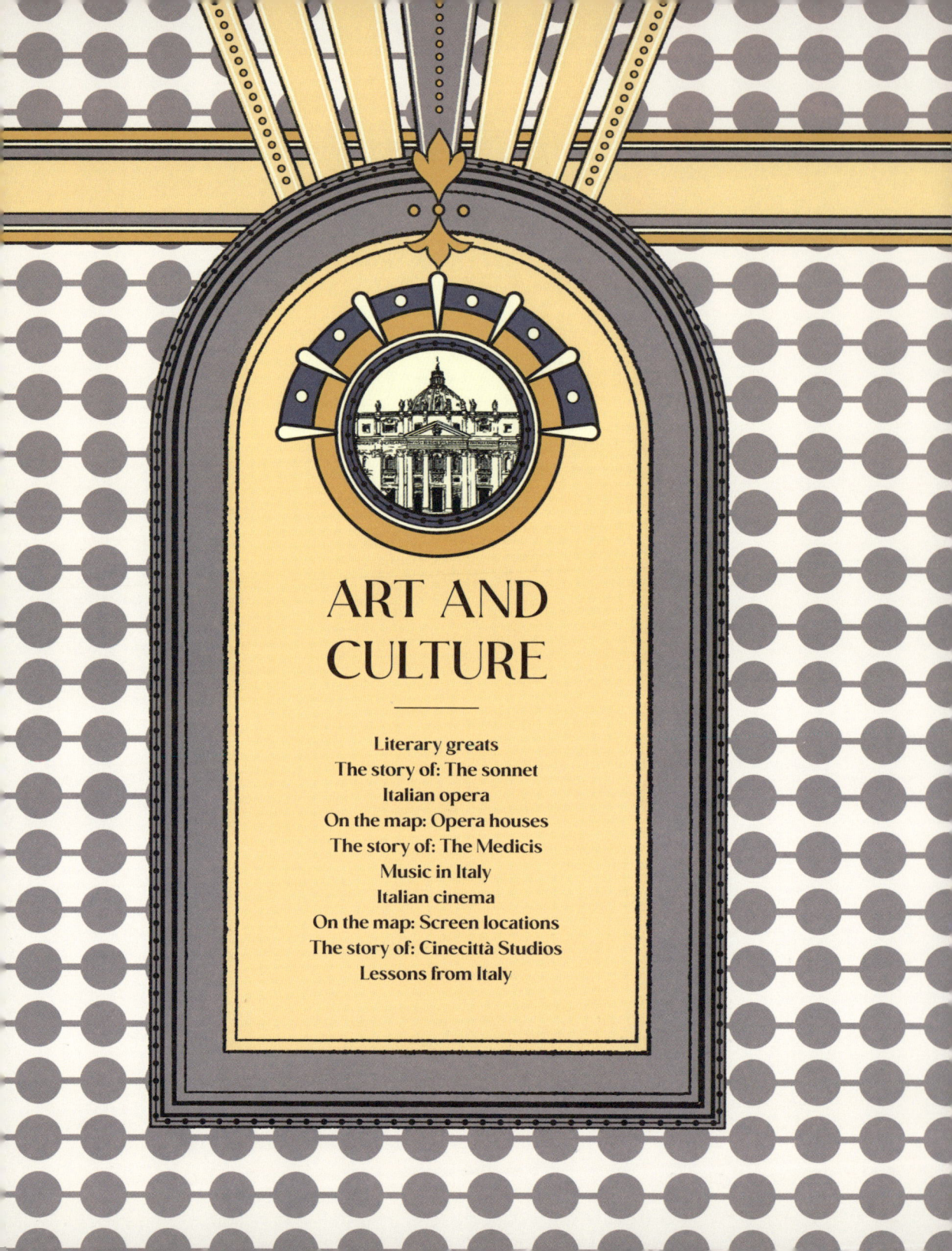

ART AND CULTURE

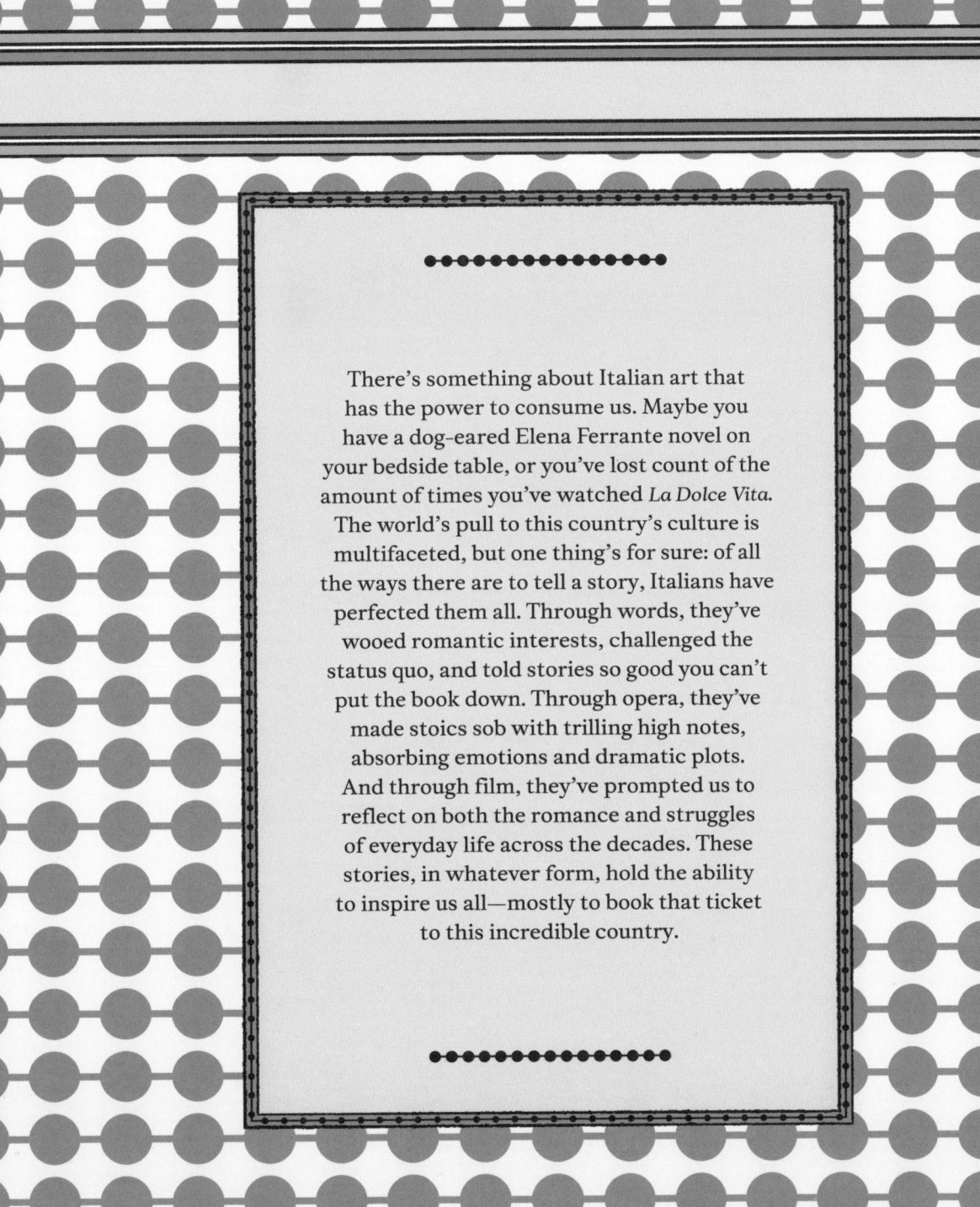

There's something about Italian art that
has the power to consume us. Maybe you
have a dog-eared Elena Ferrante novel on
your bedside table, or you've lost count of the
amount of times you've watched *La Dolce Vita*.
The world's pull to this country's culture is
multifaceted, but one thing's for sure: of all
the ways there are to tell a story, Italians have
perfected them all. Through words, they've
wooed romantic interests, challenged the
status quo, and told stories so good you can't
put the book down. Through opera, they've
made stoics sob with trilling high notes,
absorbing emotions and dramatic plots.
And through film, they've prompted us to
reflect on both the romance and struggles
of everyday life across the decades. These
stories, in whatever form, hold the ability
to inspire us all—mostly to book that ticket
to this incredible country.

LITERARY GREATS

A library full of Italian classics

"A classic is a book that has never finished saying what it has to say." So wrote Italy's most famous 20th-century writer, Italo Calvino. He could have been speaking about any number of Italy's great literary creations—from Giovanni Boccaccio's *Decameron* to Elena Ferrante's *My Brilliant Friend*—which continue to offer us new ways of thinking about love, politics, faith, and friendship. Whether penning trenchant religious sermons, writing romantic odes, or challenging the status quo through political prose, the country's writers have scraped off Italy's simple *dolce vita* surface to reveal the dark, complex, and often beautiful truths underneath.

The original romantics

For many Italian wordsmiths, there's nothing more important than love, and this passion for romantic prose can be traced all the way back to the Romans. Plenty of ancient poets (like Catullus) penned adoring verse in Latin, but it was from the medieval period that Italians composed some of the world's greatest love poetry, creating perfect new forms like the sonnet *(p193)* to capture their devotion. Few did this better than Dante Alighieri, whose early love poems collected in his famous *La Vita Nuova (The New Life)* document his romantic love for a woman named Beatrice.

While medieval courtly love poetry was largely dominated by lovesick men, the Renaissance saw women writers telling their side of the story. Gaspara Stampa—now considered the greatest female poet of the Italian Renaissance—wrote 200 fiery odes to her emotionally unavailable lover, the Venetian Count Collaltino. Where courtly love poetry was defined by strict convention, Stampa's verse questions the very tropes of romantic poetry, showing that there are as many ways of writing love as there are of feeling it.

THE STORY OF
Literature for all

It may have been the aristocracy bankrolling art and literature in the Renaissance, but the idea was that great works of art should be for everyone. Hence, the opening of libraries. The 15th-century Biblioteca Malatestiana in Cesena, central Italy, is thought to be the first library in Europe that was open to the public, as opposed to being in the hands of the Church or aristocracy.

1321

Dante completes *La Divina Commedia (The Divine Comedy)* using the Tuscan vernacular instead of Latin.

1524

Baldassare Castiglione finishes *Il Libro del Cortegiano (The Book of the Courtier).*

1538

Vittoria Colonna's *Rime* (Poetry) publishes, opening the doors for female writers.

1827

I Promessi Sposi (The Betrothed), by Alessandro Manzoni, is the first modern novel in Italian.

1947

Se Questo è un Uomo (If This Is A Man), Primo Levi's memoir of his incarceration in Auschwitz, prints.

1957

Elsa Morante becomes the first woman to win the Strega, Italy's prize for literature.

2011

Elena Ferrante publishes the first of her hugely popular *Neapolitan Quartet* novels.

● ● ●

Above Franz Xaver Winterhalter's depiction of Boccaccio's *Decameron*
Right Early 20th-century cover of Dante's *Divine Comedy*

DANTE ALIGHIERI
LA DIVINA COMMEDIA

William Shakespeare

Perhaps the greatest writer in history owes it all to Italy. William Shakespeare set 13 of his 38 plays here—partly because Italian verse was revered, and partly because he could tackle issues that would have been political hotcakes at home. Venice and Verona were two of his favorite settings.

● ● ●

Political pioneers

While some writers were swooning over the page, others were holding power to account. Italy's long history of disparate states means that politics has always been in the foreground of the country's literature, and writers have often been the driving force of social progress. This came to the fore during the Renaissance. In Florence, statesman and philosopher Niccolò Machiavelli wrote *Il Principe (The Prince)*, a kind of instruction manual for political leaders. The book completely changed the way we think about power and how it's obtained, separating politics from ethics and suggesting a certain ruthlessness is necessary to achieve our social goals. The book immediately found a wide audience, sweeping Europe and becoming one of the most influential (and misunderstood) political works of all time.

In the late 1800s and early 1900s, political writing took on a different tenor, as *verismo* (literary realism) sought to denounce the poverty that was eviscerating working-class Italy. Writers like Giovanni Verga and Grazia Deledda penned socially detailed novels, with Verga's *I Malavoglia (The House by the Medlar Tree*, 1881) exploring the harsh lives of a family of Sicilian fishers. The act of writing was seen as a form of political activism, with engaged writers committed to improving the lives of ordinary Italians after unification.

This commitment to the power of literature remains alive today. And as Italy emerged from two world wars, a prominent school of anti-Fascist writers used literature to expose the horrors of war and the injustices of oppression. Jewish-Italian chemist and writer Primo Levi survived the Holocaust and published *Se Questo è un Uomo (If This Is a Man)*, a hugely influential testimony of his time incarcerated in Auschwitz. Just like the *verismo* writers before him, Levi told his tale using stark and subtle realism, something all the more affecting given the horrors he was describing.

into Italy's tradition of innovation by probing at the boundaries between fiction and reality.

Then there's Umberto Eco, a philosopher and experimental writer who created intricately plotted mysteries in his bestselling books, from *Il Nome della Rosa* (*The Name of the Rose*) to *Il Pendolo di Foucault* (*Foucault's Pendulum*). Like Calvino, Eco had a gift for conveying complex ideas in a highly readable style, paving the way for a generation of Italian writers who show that writing complex literature doesn't mean sacrificing a wide readership.

Contemporary classics
Today, Italian authors continue to innovate, with that political edge still clearly on show. The Neapolitan novels of Elena Ferrante, whose true identity is unknown, look at poverty and crime in Naples. By exploring female friendship, corruption, and gender politics, Ferrante has global fame, leading to a phenomenon called "Ferrante fever."

Italy's seedier side has also been explored by journalist Roberto Saviano, who wrote about organized crime in his thinly veiled novel, *Gomorrah*. For over a decade, Saviano has required police protection to ensure his safety, proving that literature still has the power to evoke political responses in Italy. While it may not be changing the world as rapidly as it did in the Renaissance, it's still holding power to account.

● ● ●

Above Elena Ferrante's Neapolitan novels **Below** Libreria Acqua Alta Venezia, a bookstore in Venice

Postmodern innovation
In the 1970s and '80s, Italy's innovative writers began to rethink the way stories were told, gradually moving away from traditional narratives. Few were as successful as Italo Calvino. His postmodernist novel *Se una notte d'inverno un viaggiatore* (*If on a Winter's Night a Traveler*, 1979) addresses the reader as they work their way through the novel, while *Le città invisibili* (*Invisible Cities*, 1972) plays out as a conversation between the Mongol emperor Kublai Khan and Marco Polo. Calvino's best works tap

———— ● ————

"Le lingue per me hanno un veleno segreto."
"Languages contain a secret poison for me."

This quote is spoken by Elena Ferrante's narrator in the final volume of the *Neapolitan Quartet*. It captures Ferrante's implicit faith in the power, and danger, of language. As Italy's greatest political writers have always known, words have the power to change the world.

———— ● ————

THE SONNET

There are few poetic forms as recognizable and enduring as the sonnet, the crown jewel of Renaissance love poetry. Over the centuries, this short form—14 lines, a regular rhyme scheme, a consistent rhythm, with a "volta" (or a "turn") at its end—has been endlessly reworked to convey just about every emotion. But where did the sonnet come from, and why has it lasted so long?

The sonnet owes a lot to the 13th-century Italian writer Giacomo da Lentini, but the form as we know it was perfected by Francesco Petrarca, often known as Petrarch. Petrarch wrote *Il Canzoniere*, a sequence of poems (mostly sonnets) in which he put his lover, Laura de Noves, firmly on a pedestal. In each poem, the lovesick Petrarch uses an array of romantic metaphors to woo his love. The shortness of the form and its iambic pentameter meant the sonnet was designed to be read aloud, a perfect declaration of (often unrequited) love.

Short and simple to memorize, the sonnet became popular among Tuscan wordsmiths like Dante and soon traveled beyond the Italian court. Sir Thomas Wyatt is credited with bringing it to England through his translations of Petrarch's verse during the Elizabethan era, whereby it reached arguably its most famous practitioner, William Shakespeare, who used the form to compare his love to a summer's day (among other things). Since then, a thousand trends have come and gone, but the sonnet remains, a small but perfectly formed letter of love.

"The shortness of the form and its iambic pentameter meant the sonnet was designed to be read aloud."

Left Dante with Beatrice, the muse for Dante's *La Vita Nuova*

ITALIAN OPERA

Hitting the high notes

Is it any surprise that opera was born in Italy? This is, after all, a country with a population seemingly hard-wired for leaning into passionate highs and doubling down on dramatic lows—qualities that make for compelling performances. But to speak of opera only in emotional terms and overlook its cultural clout would be to sell this most enduring of forms short.

The birth of opera

Like many notable creations in Italy, opera began in the Medici court in Florence, just after the High Renaissance, dreamt up by a group of artists, poets, and musicians who were feeling experimental. Known as the "Camerata," this forward-thinking Florentine group was also obsessed with looking back, primarily at ancient Greek drama, which they were eager to revive. Their idea? To tell these stories through *opera in musica*, or "a work in music."

One of the group's key members was the composer Jacopo Peri, who leaned on a libretto written by his Camerata colleague Ottavio Rinuccini to help him reimagine the myth of Apollo and Daphne. Peri's resulting work, *Dafne*, is widely considered the world's first

opera and was performed at Palazzo Tornabuoni in 1598 to great success. It caught the Medici family's keen attention and, under their commission, Peri went on to compose *Euridice*, which was performed at the wedding of Maria de' Medici and Henry IV of France just two years later. During this time, the genre itself—which combined music, theater, and dance—gathered steam all around Italy, with other regions' noble courts taking cues from Tuscan shows.

Early operas

Taking on the baton from Peri was composer Claudio Monteverdi, who took the genre one step further. In 1607, he presented *L'Orfeo*, which combined all the elements that now define opera: lines delivered in perfect harmony with dramatic music, immersive artificial backdrops, and characters giving vent to extreme emotions. Commitments to show-manship were intense: this was the burgeoning period of the *castrato*, male singers who were castrated before puberty to maintain their ability to hit the high notes (and, in some cases, play female roles). Opera was becoming grander than ever before.

A form so dramatic needed a suitable home, and it wasn't long before the launch of public opera houses across Italy. No longer was opera confined to private spaces for the nobility; rather, you could buy a ticket to watch a show with the masses (albeit often at a steep price). Venice opened the first opera house, the Baroque-era Teatro San Cassiano, in 1637; by the end of the century, the city was home to 17 opera houses, and the Italian love for the form was well and truly established.

In an evolution that fits nicely with opera's broadening audience base, the over-the-top Baroque period began to give way to the more straightforward Classical period. Neapolitan opera introduced the masses to the comical *opera buffa*, a distinct genre that contrasted with *opera seria*, the model that centered around *castratos*. *Opera buffa* pulled less from sweeping "hero's journey"-style stories and more from recognizable incidents of everyday life. In a way, this relatability was the operatic equivalent of Dante writing in his native Tuscan rather than Latin; audiences were seeing characters they could identify with.

Age of the greats

This lightened touch helped diversify opera and open the door for further innovations in the 19th century. Composer Gioachino Rossini was the dominant figure of the first half of the century, equally nimble in both comic (*The Barber of Seville*) and serious (*Ermione*) opera, so much so that he broke down barriers between the two. Another giant of the genre was Giuseppe Verdi. Verdi became a key force in the Risorgimento (Italian unification movement) with his opera *Nabucco* (1846) and its rousing chorus of "Va, Pensiero." In this song, exiled enslaved Hebrews sing about their homeland, which was thought to be a thinly veiled anthem for Italian patriots. Verdi's 20th-century heir Giacomo Puccini, meanwhile, was less politically engaged than Verdi but no less effective. His operas like *Tosca* and *Madama Butterfly* were more concerned with emotional realism. Such is the power of these works that Verdi and Puccini remain household names, even among those who have never set foot inside an opera house.

●●●
Previous page left
Drawing of La Scala
Previous page right
Audiences at La Scala
Clockwise from top
Verona Arena; Poster for Verdi's *Otello*; Performance of *The Barber of Seville*

ANNA RENZI

Anna Renzi (1620–1660) was the first professional female opera singer. She rose to fame in Venice's opera houses, where Papal decrees banning women from singing weren't enforced.

THE STORY OF
The Three Tenors

Opera's favorite "supergroup," the Three Tenors (1990–2003) comprised Italian heavyweight Luciano Pavarotti and the Spaniards Plácido Domingo and José Carreras. Their varied repertoire consisted of everything from traditional classics like "Nessun Dorma" to operatic covers of songs from pop and Broadway, bringing new audiences to the world of modern opera.

Opera today

Puccini-esque emotional emphasis in opera hasn't gone anywhere, but the sociopolitical element is back, front and center in today's houses. Going to the opera isn't just about revisiting the best works of past *maestri* (though there's plenty of that, too, with events like the Rossini Festival in Pesaro, the Verdi Festival held in places dear to the *Falstaff* composer, and the Puccini Festival in Lucca). From Parma to Palermo, the country's opera houses serve as important cultural and political gathering spaces. Nowhere is this truer than at Teatro alla Scala in December, when the famous Milanese house hosts its opening night of the new season. Special invites are highly coveted, and though the night is always attended by VIPs and politicians in their red-carpet finery, it's more than a photo op. Seating arrangements of leaders in the Royal Box and murmurings (and, potentially, outbursts or acts of protest) from the crowd are widely reported on, and often help give a read of the cultural temperature at year's end. Well, it wouldn't be opera without a little drama and theatrics.

Above Backstage in costume before a show at La Scala
Right Luciano Pavarotti of the Three Tenors

PAOLO BESANA

●

On the enduring history and vast archives of La Scala

There are few opera houses as storied as Milan's La Scala. The theater's hallowed stage has hosted the finest operas by just about every great name from the first half of the 19th century and beyond: Rossini, Bellini, Donizetti, Verdi. To this day, La Scala's Opening Night, which happens every year on Sant'Ambrogio (December 7, Milan's patron saint's day), is among the most important nights in Italy's cultural calendar. Few can speak as eloquently about the theater's illustrious history—and the ways it plans to preserve this history—than La Scala's Director of Communication, Paolo Besana.

Besana's own involvement with the theater stretches back to 1992, when he first joined as an usher during his studies. He is now responsible for all facets of communication, including the theater's publishing program, the website, and, perhaps most intriguingly, La Scala's vast archive. A theater with a history this extensive is sure to have some wonders stored in its records, and that's certainly true of La Scala. "The archive contains documents, costumes, sketches for sets from some of the most important Italian artists of the 20th century, and around a million photos," says Besana. "It's

an immense, enormous treasure—digging in, we're always finding new things."

Going forward, Besana is eager to make this operatic repository more readily available. It's in the theater's nature to seek to broaden the appeal of the art form—from its earliest days, La Scala prided itself on being an institution for the people. Plans are already underway to digitize many of the treasures, making the annals of history accessible to scholars and opera fans.

But Besana is particularly excited about the costumes. For decades, the world of fashion has looked to La Scala for inspiration. "La Scala played a key role in making Milan a great city of fashion," he says, with designers like Giorgio Armani taking inspiration from the theater (they have even designed costumes for many of the theater's shows). As important is keeping all of these costumes in good knick: "The work on these costumes is mainly about restoration— they are stored in a huge old factory south of Milan; it's where our laboratories are. We are planning to move to a larger space, which will take a few years." As Besana and his team continue to unearth new riches from the archives, there's no telling what gems they might uncover.

OPERA HOUSES

Italy's first opera houses sprang up in the 17th century, and as the genre's popularity grew, so too did the demand for larger and more sophisticated theaters. Opera houses often reflect the architectural trends of their time, but what unites them all is their monumental spectacle and ability to evoke a sense of awe, before you've even heard a note. A large part of that is down to the dress code. Luxurious, shimmering costumes aren't just worn by the performers: a night at the opera means dress-to-impress, and Italy's glamorous locals don't hold back.

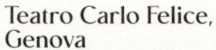

Teatro Regio, Parma

Parma residents see their city as the real home of opera and this theater, associated with local boy Verdi, as the crown jewel. They've been known to drive performers to tears with their critical reactions.

Teatro Carlo Felice, Genova

Not just an opera house but a cultural lighthouse, Carlo Felice's Rococo extravagance symbolizes the wealth of 19th-century Genova. Destroyed by bombs in World War II, it was boldly restored by architect Aldo Rossi.

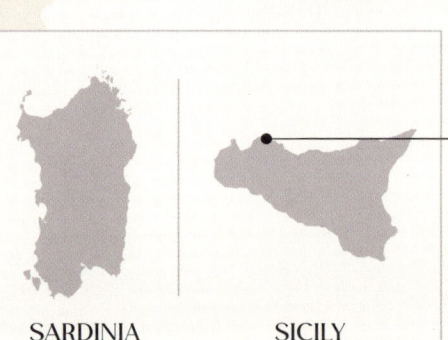

SARDINIA   SICILY

Teatro Massimo, Palermo

The third-largest opera house in Europe at the time of its inauguration in 1897, Massimo beautifully blends the Neo-Classical, Art Nouveau, and Arab-Norman architectural styles that Sicily is famous for.

La Scala, Milan

This Neo-Classical theater is one of the world's most prestigious opera houses. It's well known for its opinion-ated audience: in 2006, tenor Roberto Alagna was famously booed off the stage during a performance of *Aida*.

Verona Arena

Italians rarely like to see old buildings die, especially Roman amphitheaters. Built to stage gladiatorial contests, Verona's site has outlasted most of its peers to become one of the most sought-after opera venues.

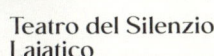

Teatro del Silenzio, Lajatico

This open-air theater is built into the Tuscan hills of Lajatico, the rural farming community where tenor Andrea Bocelli was born. It operates just once a year, for a special concert by Bocelli.

Teatro Petruzzelli, Bari

Opened in 1903 by the Petruzzelli brothers, entre-preneurs who sought to boost Bari's cultural scene, this theater is an icon of southern opera. It was destroyed in a 1991 fire but reopened in 2009.

Teatro San Carlo, Naples

The oldest still-standing opera house in the world, San Carlo was founded in 1737, when Naples was at the forefront of the operatic revolution. It's remarkably stood the test of time and remains a symbol of Neapolitan pride.

THE STORY OF
...

THE
MEDICIS

Italy's early cultural flourishing is intimately tied to one family: the House of Medici. Their story begins in 1434, when Cosimo de Medici (commonly known as Cosimo the Elder) accrued huge wealth by expanding the Florentine banking system. Then, as now, a formidable bank balance brought political clout, and Cosimo was soon controlling the levers of power in Florence.

His rise coincided with a wave of Humanist thought across Italy, as writers and thinkers praised the arts as the worthiest form of human endeavor. With his autumn years approaching and his coffers growing ever larger, Cosimo became a devoted patron of Florence's burgeoning art scene, commissioning artists such as Donatello and Fra Angelico and building vast *palazzi* and public libraries. What better way for an aging Humanist to cement his legacy? This patronage flowed down through the generations, with Cosimo's grandson, Lorenzo de Medici, funding some of the finest artists of his day—without his patronage, we may never have swooned over the works of Sandro Botticelli, Leonardo da Vinci, and Michelangelo. As if the arts weren't enough, the Medici family was to provide four popes and one Queen of France (Catherine de Medici would marry Henry II to rule France from 1547 to 1559).

The last Medici ruler died in 1737, but the family had irrevocably changed the world of European art, politics, and finance. Over the best part of 300 years of their rule, Florence was turned into Italy's cultural bedrock, a city of vast opera houses, echoing theaters, and opulent galleries.

"Cosimo de Medici became a devoted patron of Florence's burgeoning art scene."

Left The Medicis depicted in *Procession of the Magi*, Benozzo Gozzoli

MUSIC IN ITALY

The country's traditional sounds

It's no coincidence that one of Dante's descriptions of Hell was of a place with no music. Harmony, notation, scale—not to mention the violin and piano—were all invented in Italy. Visit the country and it won't take long for you to see the role music plays, as crowds line up at the concert hall and folk singers hold streetside singalongs.

Classical sounds

Italy's great composers weren't confined to the world of opera (*p194*).

INSPIRED BY ITALY

Vivaldi's concertos

Venetian composer Antonio Vivaldi (1678–1741) was instrumental in establishing one of classical music's favorite forms: the concerto, a composition for a solo instrument accompanied by an orchestra. The form spread rapidly around Europe, reinterpreted by leading composers.

● ● ●

During the Renaissance, early Italian musicians were taking sacred music to new heights by perfecting the composition of the Mass, a piece of music designed to give praise to God. Giovanni Pierluigi da Palestrina (1525-1594) was a central figure in what is now known as the Roman School. He pioneered contrapuntal composition: playing multiple melodies at once to create soaring harmonies.

That's not to say Italy's role call of composers are a thing of the past, by the way. Perhaps the most famous film composer is Italy's very own Ennio Morricone, who scored over 70 award-winning films, many of them directed by Sergio Leone. Morricone's dark sonic worlds set new standards in film music and have come to be closely associated with Spaghetti Westerns. His opening theme for *The Good, the Bad, and the Ugly* (1966) is now one of the most iconic scores in film history. Then there's Ludovico Einaudi, whose gentle, piano-driven songs and scores have added heart to countless films and TV shows, including *Nomadland* (2020) and *This Is England* (2006).

Folk traditions

And there's plenty else up Italy's sleeve. The country's disparate folk

Above Ennio
Morricone with
the Roma Sinfonietta
orchestra at the
Royal Palace of
Caserta

scene is a legacy of the cracked
mirror of pre-unified Italy, with styles
associated with particular regions.
Liscio, a kind of foxtrot, is popular in
Emilia-Romagna, but you'd struggle to
find anyone from outside the region
who's even heard of it. Likewise, many
are unaware that Abruzzo has its own
version of the bagpipes—the *zampogna*—
which forms part of the region's
music. Mandolins are ubiquitous in
Naples, but rare elsewhere.

Many popular folk songs are sung
in dialect, such as *"Oh mia bela*

Madunina," "Ma se ghe penso," and
"O sole mio," all of which have become
anthems of their respective cities
(Milan, Genova, Naples). With their
rousing choruses, evocative lyrics, and
simple structures, these songs are
designed to be sung collectively, and
you're likely to hear them belted out at
soccer matches or played on a busy
street. After all, it doesn't matter
whether it's a classical tune or a folk
song—or perhaps even Eurovision-
winning rock—Italy's musical output
has always brought people together.

ITALIAN CINEMA

Icons of the silver screen

Spectacular landscapes, great food, and gregarious people: much of the image we have in our heads of Italy as a land of *la dolce vita* is down to what we see in the theater. Yet while the sweet life ruled the screen in the 1960s and '70s, Italy's film industry isn't all glitz and glam. From Fascist propaganda movies to the haunting Neorealist movement, Italy's film canon paints a complex picture of the country. And while many films break genre boundaries and challenge the status quo, few look so good doing it as Italy's.

The early days

Italian cinema had a quiet beginning. Shortly after the Lumière brothers debuted their early films in 1895, filmmakers in Italy started experimenting. Silent films, such as *The Last Days of Pompeii* (1908) and *Cabiria* (1914), entranced audiences with their groundbreaking shots, lavish sets, and dramatic retellings of Italian history. While the talkies took over in the 1930s, ancient stories were still at the core of Italian filmmaking—and Benito Mussolini made sure of it. In order to harness the power of movies to produce his Fascist propaganda, he founded Cinecittà (a film studio near Rome). Here, the dictator funded epics such as *Scipione L'Africano* (1937), which followed ancient Roman statesman Scipio Africanus as he conquered Carthage. The films wowed large audiences and seeded Mussolini's dream of recreating the mighty Roman Empire. While Fascism later declined, Mussolini's Cinecittà (*p215*) only rose, becoming Europe's largest film studio and the epicenter of Italian cinema to come.

Neorealism emerges

Postwar Italy ushered in a new era of cinema. Destruction and poverty were

---

THE STORY OF

Elvira Notari

Italy's first known female film director was Elvira Notari, born in 1875 in Salerno. In 1906, she cofounded Dora Film and began by producing shorts shown at the end of feature films in the theater. Notari would go on to make documentaries and feature films about working-class Naples. Dora Films was shut down by Fascist authorities in 1928 for its focus on blue-collar characters—but Notari's films paved the way for Italian postwar Neorealism.

INSPIRED BY ITALY

Sounds of cinema

When Sergio Leone's *A Fist Full of Dollars* (1964) was released, cinephiles were captivated by its violence, dramatic storytelling, and melodramatic music. Leone's stylized direction transformed filmmaking across Europe and America, while Ennio Morricone's incredible score—with its guitars, harmonicas, whistles, and howls—forever changed the way movies sounded.

• • •

rife in the streets, and as a result, film-makers had little desire to tell stories about the great Roman Empire and Fascist bravado. Instead, they chose to focus on the harsh realities and every-day struggles of Italians—and with that, the Neorealistic movement was born. As Cinecittà was bombed during the war, directors shot on location and often used nonprofessional actors to amp up the realism. For example, Roberto Rossellini's *Rome, Open City* (1945) was filmed on the streets of the bombed-out capital and turned little-known actor Anna Magnani into an international star. Perhaps the most famous film to come out of this period was Vittorio De Sica's *Bicycle Thieves* (1948), which won an Academy Award for its tragic tale of a father and son in poverty. Filmmakers around the world were inspired, but audiences weren't always impressed: after the destruction of World War II, many Italians wanted escapism rather than realism. Consequently, the genre faded in the 1950s, yet the films laid the groundwork for French New Wave and American independent cinema.

The sweet life

Giving the people what they now wanted was Federico Fellini. His films were extravagant, surreal, and glamorous, the perfect antidote to Neorealism. His iconic *La Dolce Vita* (1960) gave a new name to the Italian

dream of the good life, while comedy-drama *8½* (1963) received critical acclaim. Meanwhile, other genres and directors emerged onto the scene. Spaghetti Westerns, popularized by Sergio Leone's *The Good, the Bad, and the Ugly* (1966), began to dominate the international stage, while female directors such as Lina Wertmüller (the first female director to be nominated for an Oscar, in 1977) and Liliana Cavani (director of the controversial *The Night Porter*, 1974) pushed Italian cinema into new territory.

Directors spurred on Italy's silver screen domination, but epic sets, spec-tacular costumes, and top-tier celebri-ties also played their part. The 1960s and '70s saw some of Italian cinema's most famous *divi* (stars) rise to fame. Sophia Loren, one of the most iconic Italian actors—her image still splashed across cities up and the down the country—forged a legendary on-screen partnership with Marcello Mastroianni, starring in films like *Yesterday, Today, and Tomorrow* (1963) and *A Special Day* (1977). Their chemistry embodied the new era of Italian cinema, where characters became more complex and emotionally driven. A rebuilt Cinecittà also found its time to shine, hosting big-budget productions like *Cleopatra* (1963), which brought Hollywood headliners like Elizabeth Taylor and Richard Burton to Rome.

• • •
Previous page *La Dolce Vita* film poster **Clockwise from top** Fellini and Mastroianni; Neorealistic film *Bicycle Thieves*; famed actress Sophia Loren

A modern romance

The 1980s to the late '90s saw a change to the Italian film industry, with less focus on the directors and more on cultivating Hollywood success. Retro romances that amped up the natural beauty of Italy (and Italians) became worldwide blockbusters—think 1988's *Cinema Paradiso* and 1994's *Il Postino* (which was directed by English film-maker Michael Radford but co-written with its Italian star, Massimo Troisi). Both films romanticized rural poverty and created a longing for a bucolic kind of *dolce vita*. Inspired by this romantic vision of Italy—and, perhaps, the financial success of showing it on screen—foreign directors flocked to the country, making films with Italy as the main character; both *A Room with a View* (1985) and *The English Patient* (1996) portrayed the countryside as lush and languid.

Cinema today

That's not to say that Italian directors no longer get a look in. Paolo Sorrentino, often compared to Fellini, achieved success with *The Great Beauty* (2013), which explored decadence and existentialism with opulent flair. Alice Rohrwacher also made waves with her mystical *La Chimera* (2023), which followed a motley crew of tomb-looters (so gregarious they could've been Fellini characters). Meanwhile, Luca Guadagnino, with films like *Call Me By Your Name* (2017), offers a mix of emotional depth and visual beauty, focusing on themes of desire and identity (with beautiful landscapes as a backdrop). After all, one thing remains constant in this country's film canon: Italy—whether its rich history, stunning landscapes, or complex people—is always the star.

● ● ●
Above *La Chimera*, a period comedy-drama
Right *Cinema Paradiso*, set in Sicily
Below Timothée Chalamet in *Call Me By Your Name*

SIMONA BALDUCCI

● ━━━━━ ● ━━━━━ ●

On the joys of working at Italy's storied film studio

Rome's iconic Cinecittà Studios *(p214)* are a legendary part of Italy's cinematic story, the name synonymous with a roster of eminent directors: Federico Fellini, Sergio Leone, and Martin Scorsese, to name just a few. But behind every auteur is a talented team of artists, designers, and architects who conjure entire worlds within a single studio. Simona Balducci, Head of Cinecittà's Art Department and the studio's Construction Manager, has been the visionary behind every Cinecittà set since 1999. The first woman in Europe to hold such a role, Balducci is uniquely equipped to talk about the joys—and practicalities—of Italian filmmaking.

"Almost the entire history of Italian cinema has passed across Cinecitta's stages," she says. "In the 1950s, many American movies were filmed here, so Cinecittà was called the 'Hollywood on the Tiber.' Everyone who works in movie-making dreams of getting the chance to work here at least once in their life." Even after decades working in the studio, Cinecittà's formidable legacy continues to inspire her. And beyond the studio? Balducci recognizes that Italy is a filmmaker's dream. "Across the country, you can find a world of landscapes, from the mountains to the sea. Plus, we have quality technicians and set builders." With so much talent and an abundance of natural beauty, it's little wonder Italian cinema has proved so enduringly successful.

Part of a film's magic is its ability to hide the technicalities of its production, becoming a seemingly effortless gateway to another world. Balducci knows, however, that bringing a film to life is often less about magic and alchemy and more about budget sheets and woodworking machines. "The first step is the budget—I estimate costs and time required; the second is choosing the right team and the right materials; and the last step is controlling all processing phases until delivery of the set." These processes might not sound thrilling on paper, but without Balducci's careful attention to detail, we would never have been whisked to medieval Florence (*The Decameron*, 2024) or paraded through the streets of ancient Rome (*For Those About to Die*, 2024), or mid-century Mexico (*Without Blood*, 2024). She has witnessed countless changes in her industry, but the success of Cinecittà's productions remains undimmed. And that, in itself, is a sort of magic.

SCREEN LOCATIONS

With its picturesque towns, rolling countryside, and ancient ruins, Italy can often feel cinematic—and many directors would be inclined to agree. The beautiful boot has numerous credits to its name, to the point where many feel an intimacy with the country just through having seen it on screen. From Fellini films to small-screen adaptations like *Ripley*, Italy is at turns the setting for thrilling car chases, coming-of-age tales, and action-packed historical epics. Simply put, this country is never just a blank canvas on screen.

Venice

Venice was one of the first cities in the world to be filmed, way back in 1896 for the Lumière brothers' *Panorama du Grand Canal vu d'un bateau*. Since then, a who's who of famous directors—Welles, Fellini, Spielberg—have utilized the scenic city.

Crema

The languorous scenes of Timothée Chalamet and Armie Hammer strolling, cycling, and falling in love in Crema brought this sleepy town to worldwide attention in 2017. *Call Me By Your Name* themed tours now operate in the area.

Sicily

Italian cinema found a new wave of fans with the coming-of-age story *Cinema Paradiso* (1988), filmed in the town of Palazzo Adriano, Sicily. The film's most memorable scenes—featuring the titular cinema—were all shot in central Piazza Umberto I.

Val d'Orcia

This Tuscan valley was the setting for Russell Crowe's recollections of home in *Gladiator* (2000), where it was portrayed as a rural paradise (the scenes were shot near Pienza, founded as a "Utopian city" in the 15th century).

SARDINIA   SICILY

Arezzo

This Tuscan city was the location for the classic Italian tearjerker *Life Is Beautiful* (1997). Many of the shots showcase the city's famous slanted piazza, while the Abbey of Sante Flora e Lucilla can be seen when Roberto Benigni's character falls into the arms of his eventual wife.

Atrani

This beguiling seaside town plays itself in the hit Netflix show *Ripley* (2024). Pictured in winter and in black-and-white, the town is stripped to its bare bones, heightening its stately beauty.

Matera

While this town's arid, cliffside dwellings and cobblestone streets have stood in for ancient Jerusalem on more than one occasion, notably in *The Passion of the Christ* (2004), they've also been the setting for a James Bond car chase in *No Time to Die* (2021).

Rome

If Italian cinema could be summed up in one image, it would be Marcello Mastroianni cavorting with Anita Ekberg in the Trevi Fountain in Fellini's immortal *La Dolce Vita* (1960).

THE STORY OF

•••

CINECITTÀ STUDIOS

With 3,000 films and 47 Oscar winners to its name, Cinecittà is no ordinary studio. Italian cinema was born in this sprawling space (it's the largest of its kind in Europe), and the studio continues to play an important role in filmmaking today. But it began under an unlikely patronage. Italian dictator Benito Mussolini founded the studio in 1937, under the slogan *"Il cinema è l'arma più forte"* ("Cinema is the most powerful weapon"). He used Cinecittà to pump out Fascist propaganda movies, which usually took the form of colossal historical epics.

Yet World War II changed everything. Fascism fell, Mussolini was executed, and Cinecittà was bombed; cinema needed a new direction. With no studio space, directors took to the streets and produced some of Italy's most critically acclaimed films. It wasn't long, however, before Cinecittà was reborn.

Rebuilt by the 1950s, the studio regained its eminence in spectacular style. American directors, attracted by subsidies and low labor costs, flocked here to film their own epics—big-budget productions such as *Ben Hur* (1959) and *Cleopatra* (1963) made use of the space, with elaborate sets and hundreds of extras. Other directors followed suit, including Federico Fellini and Francis Ford Coppola, who shot much of *The Godfather Part III* (1990) here. More recently, city-size sets were built in the studio for the HBO series *Rome* (2005). It would seem, then, that Cinecittà's spirit for the epic is yet to be broken.

"With 3,000 films and 47 Oscar winners to its name, Cinecittà is no ordinary studio."

Left The making of the film *Cleopatra* at Cinecittà

LESSONS FROM ITALY

Learning from the world's muse

For a nation that proudly celebrates the sweet art of doing nothing, Italy has certainly been busy. The country's influence is found all around the world, from grand public squares to the fastest cars on our highways. It's there in the finer details, too—that perfectly tailored suit, that gentle stroke of the paint brush. As we hurtle through the 21st century, with new trends emerging every day, what does Italy still have to teach us?

For one thing, Italy shows that to be pioneering doesn't mean abandoning the past. Italian tailors and seamstresses continue to hone their craft in the face of fast fashion. Creatives recognize the beauty of going full circle, as artists take their work to the streets and architects design social spaces—just like their ancient predecessors. Even car makers show that yesterday's engines can be adapted to meet the sustainable demands of tomorrow.

Indeed, there's a slowness to Italian life that offers an antidote to the pace of the modern world. Instead of buying a coffee and rushing off, we're encouraged to linger awhile as the Moka pot brews. We remember that creating a meal starts with a simple conversation at the market. And we reflect that no matter how much the world changes, it's those moments with our family and friends that we'll savor.

Going forward, Italy will continue doing its own thing in its own inimitable style. It will continue brewing coffee, slicing pizza, designing dresses, and creating art—because the good life matters here. That, in short, is the magic of the Italian way.

"The name of Italy has magic in its very syllables."

Mary Shelley

In the early 19th century, English novelist Mary Shelley was spellbound by Italy. Like millions before and after her, she was inspired to create some of her finest works while living here.

Clockwise from left
Swimming by the
Cinque Terre; Rome's
Piazza Navona; a
side street in Rome

INDEX

219

ACKNOWLEDGMENTS

DK would like to thank the following people for their contribution to this project: Darius Arya, Simona Balducci, Paolo Besana, Alessandro Boscu, Angela Caputti, Edoardo Celadon, Toni DeBella, Lindsay Gabbard, Ariane Lotti, Valeria Merlini, Alice Pasquini, Graziella Sabatini, Lucy Sara-Kelly, Serena Scoloco, Daniela Storti, and Andrea Strafile

Erica Firpo is a Rome-based culture and travel writer and founder of the award-winning digital magazine and podcast, *Ciao Bella*. When she's not uncovering Italy's hidden gems or exploring ancient ruins, she's crafting stories about art, food, and history. She contributes regularly to *AFAR*, *The Washington Post*, *Conde Nast Traveler*, *Travel + Leisure*, and *The Guardian*.

Alex Sakalis grew up between Greece and London but has called Italy home for the past seven years. He has visited all 20 Italian regions, over half the provinces, and is working towards his goal of cycling every valley on the southside of the Alps. He is a staff writer for *Italy Magazine*, where he contributes articles on travel, architecture, history, and culture.

Mary Gray is an American journalist and editor who's been reporting from Italy for English-speaking audiences for over a decade. Currently the editor-in-chief of *Italy Magazine*, she's been spotlighted by Italian newspaper *Repubblica* for her contributions to international media about Florence. Mary has also covered literature for *The Washington Post*, slept in Puglia's masserie on assignment for *Qantas Travel Insider* and, in a career peak, once saw her Italian food writing publicly praised by Italian cook Marcella Hazan's widower.

Liz Shemaria is an Italy-based journalist. Her writing has been published in *BBC Travel*, *AFAR*, and Fodor's. Aside from her travels to Italy's 20 regions, her quest for the unfamiliar has led to trekking solo in Himalaya, picking prickly pears in Puglia, and chanting sutras on sacred Mount Minobu in Japan.

Laura Rysman is an American journalist and longtime resident of Italy, currently living in Florence. A frequent contributor to *The New York Times* and *Monocle*, she is usually crisscrossing Italy in search of little-known destinations, great meals, and stories.

Vanessa Mulquiney is a Rome-based travel writer and editor. A former *Time Out* city editor, her work has appeared in publications such as *The Telegraph*, *The Australian*, *Forbes Travel Guide*, *Going Places*, Tripadvisor, and *Vogue*.

Phoebe Hunt moved from London to Italy in her twenties and never looked back. She's been an au pair, done a stint in a Tuscan restaurant, and posed for Renaissance-style paintings, but mostly she works as a travel journalist. When she's not hosting her own supper clubs, she writes for *Time Out*, *Suitcase*, and *National Geographic*, and has co-authored various DK books, including *Florence Like a Local*.

Julia Buckley is a Venice-based journalist who writes about Italy for UK and US publications including the *Times*, *CNN*, and *National Geographic*. A former travel editor on UK newspapers, she has also contributed to guidebooks on Italy for DK and Lonely Planet and loves nothing more than a road trip through rural Italy or a high-speed train ride down the peninsula.

PICTURE CREDITS

4Corners: Antonino Bartuccio 83br; Matteo Carassale 118tr, 131tl; Colin Dutton 104bl; Günter Gräfenhain 201clb; Giuseppe Greco 54clb; Lisa Linder 118br; Frank Lukasseck 140br; Luca Da Ros 134tr; Alessandro Saffo 81tl; Marco Simoni 134tl.

Alamy Stock Photo: Agenzia Sintesi / Fiorani Fabio 109br; AGTravel 76cl; Album / Miramax / Strizzi, Sergio 213tl; Alexblacksea 179tc; Allstar Picture Library Ltd 208–209tc; Associated Press / Anonymous 159; Avpics 171tr; Georg Berg 165tc; BFA / Neon 210tr; Philip Bird 212crb; Stuart Black 123l; Blue Robin Collectables 207; Paolo Bona 198tr; Mario Carovani 121tc; CFphotos 165bc; Cola Images 169tl; Matthew Corrigan 37t; DPA Picture Alliance Archive 197bl; Andrew Duke 40cl; Julian Eales 129tl; © Adam Eastland 184cl; Adam Eastland 183; EmmePi Travel 111tl; 201tr; Ermes.S 170clb; Everett Collection Inc 208br; Eversummer 161t; Andrea Federici 108br; Kirk Fisher 101br; FlixPix 208clb; Andrew Fox 136–137; funkyfood London - Paul Williams 86cb; Rebeca Sendroiu Gilcescu 98cl; Alberto Grosescu 161br; Jacob Halls 124tl; Hemis / Maisant Ludovic 181cra; Hemis / Serrano Anna Courtesy of Zaha Hadid Architects 181bc; Hemis.fr / René Mattes 103bl; Heritage Image Partnership Ltd 175bc; Heritage Image Partnership Ltd / © Fine Art Images 189t; Peter Horree 202–203; Stephen Hughes 99; Image Professionals GmbH / Ingolf Pompe 109tr; Image Professionals GmbH / Sabine Lubenow 196–197tc; incamerastock / ICP 40–41t; Independent Photo Agency Srl 121crb; Wieslaw Jarek 213cra; LaPresse / Gianluca Moggi 201ca; Lifestyle pictures 210br; Alberto Masnovo 48cr; mauritius images GmbH / ClickAlps 52bc; mauritius images GmbH / Steffen Beuthan 54bc; Julie Mayfeng 195; Annapurna Mellor 123cra; Trinity Mirror / Mirrorpix 198br; Motoring Picture Library / National Motor Museum 169c; Francesco Mou 108cl; Sawassakorn Muttapraprut 95tl; Eric Nathan 39; North Wind Picture Archives 37b; Ollirg 81bl; PAINTING 42; Paolo Reda - REDA &CO 87bc; Paolo Reda - REDA &CO / Eddy Buttarelli 180cb; Photo 12 172–173; Pictorial Press Ltd 170bc; Prisma Archivo 194t; Jussi Puikkonen 103tl; Realy Easy Star 34–35, 197br; robertharding / Eleanor Scriven 13cr; Grant Rooney - Palio di Siena Collection 145bc; Kay Roxby 191tl; salla_dinho 87tc; Peter Schickert 164c; Steve Tulley 82tr; United Archives GmbH / IFA Film 210cr; United Archives GmbH / Impress 213bc; Universal Images Group North America Llc / DeAgostini / Dea / M. Leigheb 155tl; Vespasian 150bl; Art Villone 189bc; Sara White 124bl, 170cla; Tim E White 104tl; Wietse Michiels Travel Stock 121clb; World History Archive 40bc; Susan Wright 112–113; Y.Levy 52tl; Konrad Zelazowski 200crb, Zoonar GmbH / Gianfranco Atzei 145cb.

AWL Images: Jon Arnold 2, 126–127; Marco Bottigelli 7; ClickAlps 4–5, 49cr, 56–57; Michele Falzone 133; Hemis 103cra, 155tr; Francesco Iacobelli 33bl, 105tl, 106bc; Maurizio Rellini 217cra; Emilia Romagna 200cb; Catherina Unger 93br.

Bridgeman Images: Sandro Chia (b.1946) / Italian / Christie's Images © Sandro Chia / VAGA at ARS, NY and DACS, London 2024. / © DACS 2024 176, G. Dagli Orti / © NPL - DeA Picture Library 23br, Raffaele Giannetti (1832-1916) / Italian 192–193; © NPL - DeA Picture Library 26br.

Depositphotos Inc: MaykovNikita Magis S.r.l. 178t.

Dreamstime.com: Anastasiya Alforova 10; Grazziela Bursuc 98br; Sebastiano Leggio 141tl; Rndmst 139tl; Francesca Sciarra 139bl; Vividaphoto 73cra; Vladimir Yudin 78ca.

Getty Images: AFP / Gabriel Bouys 141br, 162tl; Richard Sellers / Allstar 150–151ts; Contour RA / Daniel Dorsa 177tl; Corbis Documentary / Atlantide Phototravel 15; Corbis Documentary / Vanni Archive 31tl; DigitalVision / Gary Yeowell 13t; DigitalVision / Henrik Sorensen 118cl; DigitalVision / Solskin 98tr, 117; DigitalVision / Thomas Barwick 86cr, 166–167, Gamma-Rapho / Victor Virgile 160br; Hulton Archive / Print Collector / CM Dixon 26cl, Hulton Archive / Umberto Cicconi 214-215; Hulton Fine Art Collection / Fine Art Images / Heritage Images 44–45, imageBROKER / Moritz Wolf 31tr; LightRocket / Marco Cantile 205; Moment / Francesco Riccardo Iacomino 18, 101tr; Moment / IanZ 29; Moment / mikroman6 16clb; Moment / Sergio Amiti 81cr; Moment / Simone Celeste 63b; Mondadori Portfolio 120cb; Mondadori Portfolio / Archivio Marilla Sicilia / Marilla Sicilia 142tr; Roger Viollet Collection 204clb; Sygma / william karel 208tl; Universal Images Group / Universal History Archive 150cl; Daniele Venturelli 144crb.

Getty Images / iStock: Antiqueimgnet 85tc; Azoor Photo Collection 175tl; Bitter 46ca, 152ca, 211tc; Yujie Chen 12; ChiccoDodiFC 84tr; Seb Coman 82–83tc; Danielkrol 165cla; DigitalVision / Ableimages 97; DigitalVision Vectors / Clu 119tc; DigitalVision Vectors / GeorgePeters 107tc; DigitalVision Vectors / ilbusca 19tc; DigitalVision Vectors / Ivan-96 163tc; E+ / 4FR 48cl, E+ / deimagine 134bc; E+ / DieterMeyrl 13bc, E+ / FilippoBacci 88–89, E+ / franckreporter 68tr; E+ / katleho Seisa 92tr; E+ / MStudioImages 95tr; E+ / Neyya 145tl; E+ / NicolasMcComber 124crb; E+ / Oleh_Slobodeniuk 217l; E+ / Pekic 123br; encrier 68tl; fatos pur 139cr;

FilippoBacci 63t; Flory 23bl; Georgeclerk 170–171t; Ilyalisse 145cra; JayBoivin 76tl; JonaVer 20; Karisssa 87ca; Kluva 199tc; Darko Lazarevic 25; lightkitegirl 71tc; Avril Morgan 17tl; mr-fox 54tr; mushroomstore 55tc; Victoria Oliynyk 114ca; PauloResende 26tr; piola666 111cr; Sophie Rabian 21cr; Fausto Riolo 27crb; SalvoV 32c; Spirins 60br; Terriana 143tc; Tunart 217br; unknown1861 64–65.

Shutterstock.com: AnSuArt 186ca; Betacam-SP 43tc; Anastasia Bielokon 190–191bc; Kristi Blokhin 91; Carolina2009 30–31b; Jon Chica 40tl; ChiccoDodiFC 73tl; Collection Maykova 75; © Michelangelo Pistoletto / Courtesy of the artist and Luhring Augustine, New York 175cr; Addolorata D'Onofrio 70tl; fansquaresss 131cr; Marija Krcadinac 131b; David A Litman 164crb; Massimo1g Calatrava Valls Santiago / © DACS 2024 184c; MC Mediastudio Bosco Verticale projected by Boeri Studio 184tl; Dima Moroz 76–77t; Morphart Creation 10ca; Moving Moment 103br; MyVideoimage 72c; Alexandre Rotenberg 124–125t; Marco Rubino Quinn Lorenzo / © DACS 2024 181tc; ValerioMei 33ca; Henk Vrieselaar 111bl; wyemji 73bl; zedspider 49bl.

Unsplash: Bjorn Agerbeek 8, Elisaveta Bunduche 72br; Marco Calignano 156–157, Louis Charron Koolhaas Rem / © OMA / © DACS 2024 180cr; Rémi Jacquaint 149, Jerry Kavan 129br, Thijs Kennis 49tl, Klemens Köpfle 190tl; Andreea Măhălean 106tr; Ellena McGuinness 58; Gonzalo Mendiola 17tr; Oriel Mizrahi / @orielmiz 130; Giuseppe Mondi 67; Tamal Mukhopadhyay 21bl; Ovidiu 61; Davide Pirotta 68–69b; reisetopia 33tr; Viviana Rishe 59br; Giordano Rosson 60tr; Anton Shcherbakov 21tl; Sir. Simo 70tr; Peter Thomas 52–53t; Ruth Troughton 146–147; Will Truettner 51; Benjamin Voros 60cl.

Cover images: Front: **Dreamstime.com:** Vladimir Yudin tr; **Getty Images** / **iStock:** Bitter bl, tl, Victoria Oliynyk ftr; **Shutterstock.com:** AnSuArt br, Morphart Creation ftl; *Back:* **Dreamstime.com:** Vladimir Yudin tr; **Getty Images** / **iStock:** Bitter tl, bl, Victoria Oliynyk ftr; **Shutterstock.com:** AnSuArt br, Morphart Creation ftl.

MIX
Paper | Supporting responsible forestry
FSC™ C018179

This book was made with Forest Stewardship Council™ certified paper—one small step in DK's commitment to a sustainable future. Learn more at www.dk.com/uk/information/sustainability

A note from the publisher
While every effort has been made to ensure this book is accurate and up to date, world events and trends can change rapidly. So if you've noticed we've got something wrong or left something out, we want to hear about it. Please get in touch at travelguides@dk.com

Senior Editor Zoë Rutland
Editor Alex Pathe
US Senior Editor Jennette ElNaggar
Project Designer Sarah Pyke
Designer Cristina Antequera
Proofreader Kathryn Glendenning
Indexer Helen Peters
Picture Researcher Marta Bescos
Senior Cartographic Editor James Macdonald
Publishing Assistant Simona Velikova
Jacket Illustrator and Illustrations Beth Mathews
Image Retouching Michelle Brier
Senior Production Editor Tony Phipps
Senior Production Controller Samantha Cross
Managing Art Editor Gemma Doyle
Editorial Director Hollie Teague
Art Director Maxine Pedliham
Publishing Director Georgina Dee

First American Edition, 2025
Published in the United States by DK Publishing,
a division of Penguin Random House LLC
1745 Broadway, 20th Floor, New York, NY 10019

Copyright © 2025 Dorling Kindersley Limited
25 26 27 28 29 10 9 8 7 6 5 4 3 2 1
001–349285–Jun/2025

A catalog record for this book
is available from the Library of Congress.
ISBN 978-0-5939-6862-8

Printed and bound in China

www.dk.com